CHRISTIANITY

RECONSIDERED

Warren L. Bowles

Also by Warren L. Bowles

Signpost to Freedom:
A Pro-Torah Commentary on the Book of Galatians

CHRIS✝IANITY

REC✡NSIDERED

Published by
Montgomery-Porter Publishing

montgomeryporter@aol.com
Denver, Colorado, U.S.A.

ISBN 978-0-9799460-0-4

Printed in USA

To Randy,
my son, in whom I am well pleased.

Contents

Introduction

This book you hold in your hands is sort of a retracing of my steps of the last few years. It is not intended in any way to be offensive or confrontational to those who are still in the Church, although I realize that the very nature of the material presented in the following pages will be taken as such by some. There are some very difficult facts to face, some which may even shake your faith. If you are a Christian who is convinced that what you know is the truth, know this: I, too, was where you are.

I was raised in a Christian home and "accepted Jesus into my heart" at the age of eleven. By the time I was seventeen, I knew that God had a call on my life to be in some type of ministry, so I began to prepare myself as best I could. I began to seriously study the Bible, learning Greek from some seminary textbooks my brother-in-law gave me, reading commentaries and any other Bible reference materials I could get my hands on.

After several years I felt I had a good grasp on the message of the Bible and was familiar with both the Old and New Testaments. Living in the northern part of British Columbia, there were no Bible colleges within hundreds of miles, so I tried some correspondence courses to further my chances of being ready for the ministry. In my late twenties, we moved to the suburbs of Vancouver, B.C., and I was able to enrol in Bible College and get my diploma. Even before I had graduated, I had been teaching adult Bible classes and was asked to serve as associate pastor at the church we were attending.

Please don't take this short history of my Christian life as bragging about how good a Bible student I was. My purpose for recounting it is to say that with all of the studying, reading, schooling and teaching I had done, the information you are (hopefully) about to read was virtually unknown to me. Many of the verses cited are ones I had committed to memory, some from a very young age. Others are ones I had taught on or had studied; all of them are verses I knew were in the Bible and I had read them countless times. Yet I never saw what I see now.

All of my life as a believer, I was sure I knew what the Bible said, and so I approached it from that perspective and just reinforced my beliefs. My preconceived ideas and pre-drawn conclusions about the Bible and its message had become a 'filter' through which I understood what it said. It wasn't until I was forty that someone suggested to me that maybe my filter was 'clogged' and I should get a new one.

Changing a 'brain filter' is much more difficult than changing an oil filter or a furnace filter, if for no other reason than it's at least easy to see when your furnace filter is dirty, unlike your brain filter. Of course, the first step in changing a mind filter is to realize that it might need to be changed; that is the hard part. For me, the realization that I needed to change my filter came after I had set out to prove that I *didn't* need to change it! Believe me, I know how hard it is to let go of ideas that you have grown up with all your life, or ones that have been faithfully taught at church every Sunday for years.

All I ask is that you read with an open mind and heart. Weigh the evidence presented before coming to your verdict. There is an old saying (I think it came from a movie) that says, "If you love something, set it free. If it comes back, it's yours; if not, it never was." Apply this principle to your ideas about your faith and your God. Disassociate yourself from them so that you can examine them more objectively. If they pass examination, then you can pick them up and hold tightly to them, knowing they are true. If, however, they are found to be faulty, then let go and seek something that can stand the test. There is no shame in discarding erroneous beliefs; the shame is in knowing they are erroneous and holding to them anyway. Those who want to find truth will find it; those who don't will never look.

I also need to add this word of caution before you embark on reading this book. If you become convinced that what I have presented is true, then you must make a decision, and the *only* acceptable decision is to bring your life into line with what the Word says. You are better off to not know the truth than to know it and live contrary to it. But this is the difficult part: if you decide to follow the instructions within the *whole* Bible, you will soon find yourself in confrontation with your Christian friends and family. You will be branded as a heretic, people will say you have joined a cult, you will be ostracized by some of your friends, you will be misunderstood, ridiculed and slandered by those whom you love now. And, if you are a pastor or work for a ministry of some kind, chances are high that you will lose your position. In short, it will not be easy to walk contrary to centuries of Christian traditions. But having said that, I must also say that the price will be worth it.

May you find that to be true.

Shalom,
Warren Bowles
Kelowna, B.C.
2003

Chapter One
So What's to Reconsider?

"I can't find anything wrong with what you're saying, Warren; it's just that you're on a different trajectory than the rest of us, so I'm going to have to ask you to resign your position as pastor of the church in Kelowna."

It took a moment for the words to sink in to my consciousness. I had come to this meeting today with the president of our denomination with mixed feelings. I had expected him to say those words, but I really was hoping he wouldn't. I was beginning to have some impact on the church, and lives were being changed. Yet my wife, Pamela, and I knew when we decided to take this step of faith that someday, sooner or later, this day would arrive; we just didn't expect it so soon.

It wasn't easy to make the decision. It went against everything I had ever learned in the Church, from the time I was a little boy in Sunday school right up through Bible College and beyond. Yet there was something that continued to draw us to this unfamiliar way. The Bible began to come alive to us as never before; many of our long-standing questions were being answered. We began to experience the blessings of God in a whole new measure. We wanted to share what we had discovered with everyone. We couldn't imagine why anyone wouldn't want to know about it too. We soon found out.

Decisions are the factors that determine our destiny. Our lives can be described as a continuous parade of minor choices punctuated with an occasional decision of such magnitude that our lives are significantly affected. There have been times when a seemingly minor decision has proved to have had major repercussions in someone's life, but those are typically an exception to the rule. Like switches on a railroad track, some decisions can merely divert us onto a parallel line for a short distance before we arrive at a junction where we would have been had we not taken the option. Others can take us to entirely different destinations. Those decisions are best made cautiously and as well-informed as possible.

The purpose for this book is to share with you one of these life-altering decisions in my life, and the process and reasoning I went through to arrive at it, in hopes that it may inspire you to make, or at least consider, the same choice. Whether or not you agree with my conclusion is, of course, your prerogative, but to render your verdict without evaluating all the evidence is to remain with the side of tradition rather than search for truth.

I want to make it clear that in reconsidering and eventually leaving Christianity, I am not taking a stance against Christians. Some of my best friends are sincere Christians who are living their lives as best they know how. They are committed to following the teachings and principles taught by the Church. What I *am* taking a stance against is the system of Christianity itself that has been carefully formulated and sustained over the centuries. That system, regardless of which denomination you pick, considers itself the bastion of truth and above question. All who raise concerns about theological issues or practices are shunned, disposed of and then discredited. Having been in pastoral ministry, I know there are unanswerable questions which cause discomfort and uneasiness; when those topics are broached, the solution is to revert to defense mechanisms rather than validate the question and search out the answer.

The truth is that pastors are taught in seminary or Bible College a perception of what the Bible says. Metaphorically speaking, they are given the lines within which they have to color. Of course, the professors and teachers were given the same lines as were *their* instructors, etc., etc., etc. It is this succession of regurgitation that has sustained the system of 'orthodoxy;' unfortunately, it has also stifled the courage of many who would question the conclusions of their forerunners. After all, if one wishes to make a career of preaching and teaching—hoping to rise through the ranks of Christendom to a place of influence and stature—then building upon the former foundation is the proper channel, not scrutinizing it. In the following pages I will attempt to expose the system from which I have removed myself. I have done so after discovering that Christianity has weighed anchor from its original moorings and has set its course contrary to the directions of the One Whom they claim to follow.

The appropriate title of the expression of faith I have come to espouse is *Messianic Judaism.* I have a Jewish friend who is not a believer in Yeshua, and he told me that "all Judaism is Messianic," meaning that true Judaism has a hope and focus on the future arrival of Messiah. While that may be true, it is not the usual meaning associated with the term. 'Messianic Judaism,' as I have come to understand it and incorporate it into my life, is simply **the Judaism that was practiced by Messiah.** Orthodox Judaism, as it is practiced around the world today, is based more upon the Talmud than the *Torah.* The Talmud is a collection of wisdom from the ancient rabbis and sages as it applies to everyday life. That wisdom is based on the *Torah,* i.e., the first five books of the Bible, and the Hebrew Scriptures, but basically falls into the category of commentary. There is much valuable insight within its pages, but it is not authoritative. While Yeshua (Jesus' real Hebrew name) walked the earth, He continually raised the ire of the religious leaders in Israel because He refused to follow or give credence to many of 'the traditions of the elders'—that body of rules and regulations later compiled as the Talmud. He always made a distinction between God's instructions for His people and man's addenda to those instructions. What He lived by and observed was the *Torah.* It was the foundation for all His teaching, and He said the purpose for which He was sent was "to fulfil the *Torah* and the Prophets,"[1] i.e., to interpret them correctly by word and deed.

However, as with Christianity, there is a broad spectrum of expression even among those who label themselves as Messianic believers. I have become aware of many 'Messianic' congregations that do not see the necessity of *Torah* observance beyond recognition of the Sabbath. They have incorporated a few Jewish-sounding and -looking things into their worship services on the Sabbath, but for the most part they remain Christian

---

[1] Matt. 5:17

churches that meet on Saturday. As I will endeavour to explain on the following pages, I have come to see that Christianity and Messianic Judaism—the Judaism that Messiah practiced—are incompatible on virtually every major point. There is a veritable chasm between the two positions and one cannot stand with one foot on each bank, so to speak.

What WOULD 'Jesus' do?

I have wondered on many occasions about the thinking of people who sport the recently popularised WWJD logo, intended to remind the wearer, 'What would Jesus do?' Do they have any idea what He would do? On what are they basing their conclusions or assumptions regarding His supposed actions? Many with whom I've come in contact seem to think that He would do pretty much the same things that they, themselves, do. But is that a true verdict on the Son of God we read about in the Bible? Just the other day I was reading through a Christian bookseller's catalogue and I came across a book with an intriguing variation on the theme. It is entitled, *What Would Jesus Eat?* A very good question that will hopefully give people some food for thought at the very least (pun intended).

The truth is that Yeshua would do very few of the things His alleged followers think He would. Recently I read an article forwarded to me by a friend via the Internet in which the writer stated flatly that Yeshua would not likely be welcome in the majority of Christian churches. Chances are He would show up on Saturday anyway, so the janitor might be the only person He got to talk to. The common Christian understanding is that Yeshua was dead-set against Judaism so He started something totally new. In reality, the Gospels portray Him as participating in much of the culture that Judaism had shaped, but He drew the line at *sola Scriptura*.[2] It is that same line which motivates me to

---

[2] Latin for 'Scripture alone.' This term was one of the main points in Martin Luther's systematic theology. He used it to imply that the Scriptures are the only authority for man seeking salvation and in matters of the Church, thereby denouncing the traditions of the Roman Catholic Church.

write this book. Had our spiritual ancestors truly re-established that distinction at the time of the reformation, the Church would be much different than it is today.

My own personal experience is also testimony as further evidence for the incompatibility of Christianity and Messianic Judaism. After spending considerable time researching and studying the contemporary validity of Messianic Judaism (including about a year of trying to disprove it because I didn't want it to be true), I became convinced and began to incorporate some of my findings into my sermons on Sunday mornings. I began slowly at first, bringing the Scriptures to light with some of the gems I had discovered while investigating the Hebrew background of the Bible. Gradually, I began to include some things that challenged the people with issues that required a modification of their lifestyles to bring them in line with the teaching of the *whole* Bible, showing how the writers of the New Testament only built on the solid foundation that Moses and the prophets had laid.

It took a while, but eventually they began to catch on to what I was really saying. In my heart, I felt that this message was the truth that could radically change the Church, and I wanted to begin with my congregation, then my denomination and beyond. I had read how Martin Luther had set out with a similar vision—to *reform* the Roman Catholic Church, not start something new.[3] But before long, I was being questioned by my superiors regarding my new direction. I soon learned that what I had found could not be mixed with Christianity; it is an either/or premise.

Although Luther had the sword of *sola Scriptura* flashing in his hand, it was that same sword that was turned against him by the Roman Catholic Church to cut away the façade of his faulty theology. As time has borne witness, a reformation of the Catholic Church is all his efforts produced. The result is a combination of the new with the old, a combination that I will elaborate on in the following pages. Had he taken the stance of total incompatibility between his revelation and the practices of

---

[3] Hence the name 'the Reformation' to that period of Church history.

the Papacy, things would be different today. It is for this reason I also wish to 'sound the alarm' as it were, to keep Messianic Judaism from becoming just a reformation of Christianity rather than the reawakening of Judaism it is supposed to be. I suppose you might call this my version of Luther's "95 Theses."

Why you haven't heard this before

As you read through the following chapters, you are likely to find yourself asking one, or both, of the following questions: "Why haven't I heard any of this before?" or "Are you saying that my pastor has been lying to me for all these years?" These are the typical responses I get when I have a chance to share some of this information with one who is unfamiliar with it. As a former pastor, I can give you some insight into the answers.

The first question is probably the most common, especially among those who have been in the Church for most of their lives. Part of the answer is covered previously in this chapter when I said that the majority of pastors just continue to teach what they were taught. They focus on repackaging the same material without questioning its validity. Many of them have never heard nor looked into this information because it is 'outside the lines' of orthodox Christianity. As far as the second question goes, I'll leave it up to you to make the ruling on that after you have considered another point of view.

One aspect of the reason behind both questions is probably more of the root issue than most pastors will admit to. Whether they have or haven't heard of this knowledge, the sad truth is that Christianity has become a money-making enterprise and this isn't a 'best seller.' That may be a rather blunt way to put it, but there is no doubt in my mind of its veracity.

Ever since the first pastor was being paid for leading a congregation, the door has been open wide for compromise to infiltrate Christianity. It works like this: A pastor's salary is dependent on money being given by the members of the local church. If for any reason the general income of the church goes down, the pastor's income can possibly be affected. The usual way to keep revenues up in the average church is to keep people in the seats and encourage them to give to 'the work of the Lord.' The way to keep people in the seats is to tell them what they want to hear. (There are some congregations that want to hear truth that challenges their lifestyle, but they are the exceptions to the rule.) Even if the pastor knows of issues within the congregation that are detrimental to the overall spiritual climate of the church, he will most likely not confront them and cause possible repercussions.

Many denominations follow what is known as the 'congregational style' of organization which means that the pastor actually works for the congregation via an appointed or elected board of representatives. Some variations have a yearly 'vote of confidence' by the general membership, others do it on a 'when the need arises' basis. Either way, the pastor always has it in the back of his mind. Considering that the vast majority of pastors have no other careers or marketable skills to fall back on, they tend to be rather protective of their job. Put yourself in their shoes; how would *you* like to have dozens or maybe hundreds of people who could affect your employment to the point where you could be terminated because they don't like what you say?

On top of this, add the enormous costs of the daily operation of one of those big church buildings and/or the mortgage that has to be paid monthly. The bottom line is that pastors have to be successful businessmen in order to keep the church afloat.

Another trap into which churches today have fallen by the hundreds is to keep people in the seats and keep new people coming in by entertaining them. The children's/youth programs have to be trendy and exciting; the music team has to be 'top notch;' the soloists have to be near 'recording artist' quality; the pastor has to be an orator, using just the right blend of humour and pathos, capable of holding your attention for twenty or even thirty (!) minutes. And all of this has to be delivered in a one-hour time slot so people can go and enjoy the rest of the day. We were once visiting some friends in a large Canadian city and went to church with them on Sunday morning. The senior pastor was in the middle of doing a series of interviews with the various members of his staff so the congregation could get to know them and what each of them did. The particular morning we were there, the young man whose turn it was to be interviewed said that his title was 'the Pastor of Platform Production.' For some reason I wasn't surprised to find out that church had come to having 'pastors' to run the productions.

Much of what is done in the Church is justified by the leaders by saying that "if Jesus were alive today, this is how He would do it." He would make use of every high-tech method and piece of equipment available; He would be doing satellite video, on-line Internet audio, etc. Maybe so, but He wouldn't do it at the cost of the message. In far too many churches, the method dictates the message.

When I found myself looking down the barrel of the 'unemployment gun' because of what I had been teaching my congregation, I didn't panic and cave in to the party line just to keep my job. We knew that this was the truth and that God would provide for our needs. I was a carpenter/cabinetmaker before I got into 'the [official, paid] ministry' and have been doing that since I got out of 'the ministry,' and He has always been faithful to us. Even if I hadn't had a trade to fall back on, we wouldn't have changed our minds. The price of just staying in the system is far higher than mere money.

Now that I have stated the basic explanations of the belief system I have left and where my journey has led me, let me share with you what I discovered when I began to investigate the foundations of the Church. These are the reasons why I left Christianity to become a Messianic believer.

Part One

Charting the Drift of Christianity

Chapter 2
From Israel to the Church

The tie with Israel

One of the cornerstones upon which I see the true message of Yeshua resting is the recognition of and association with Judah/Israel.[1] Today there is a growing movement among Christianity that recognizes the Jews/Israel as God's chosen people. Rallies, conferences, etc., are held to raise awareness of the plight of Israel and the Jews around the world. There are Christian organizations that endeavour to involve themselves in fulfilling the prophecies about aiding the Jews to return to their land. Many see this as a commendable gesture by these largely non-Jewish organizations that wish to bless the Jews.[2] It is certainly wise from the standpoint of knowing that Yeshua Himself described a time to come when He will judge the nations based upon their treatment of the Jews.[3] It is also far superior to the attitude fostered by the Church for centuries and even embraced by many Christians today: that God's purpose for Israel ended with Yeshua, and, in fact, the Jews are now to be despised because they are the enemies of God since they are 'the Christ killers.' Nothing could be further from the truth! That Yeshua was to be rejected and killed was foreordained from the beginning.[4] It was because Israel rejected Him that salvation was

---

[1] Since being released from captivity in the 6th century BCE, the people of Israel have been called 'Jews' as a nickname for 'Judah,' the leading tribe of the kingdom called by the same name.

[2] Some question the 'carte blanche' approach taken by many of these groups. Estimates of the number of non-Jewish people being brought into Israel range as high as 60%, and the percentage of atheists/secular people is much higher than that. There is concern among the believers in Israel that unless there is a drastic change in those figures, a third expulsion from the land may happen to the people of Israel for the same reason as the first two: unfaithfulness to their covenant with God.

[3] Matt. 25:31-46, Israel/the Jews are never considered to be one of 'the nations.' 'The nations' in Scripture always refers to all the nations *except* Israel. The difference between sheep and goats, i.e., those who will be blessed or cursed for eternity, is their actions toward "the least of these *My brethren*."

[4] See John 10:18; 12:27; Ac. 2:23

made available to non-Jews. We should *thank* them, not despise them. It was from such an attitude that 'replacement theology' arose, i.e., the idea that the Church has now *replaced* Israel in God's plan.

The position enjoined and supported by the Bible is that we should identify *with* Israel. The Church is not a replacement of her, nor is it a companion to her, as one who is along side of her. True believers are now "brought near," made "fellow citizens," no longer "aliens from the covenants of promise." We are "grafted in"—part of the same tree; we are part of "one new man" made from Jew and non-Jew. People ask me why I wear a *tallit* (prayer shawl). Is it Scriptural? No, except for the tassels on the four corners of the *tallit*. Why do I wear one? Identification. If I have joined their family, there should be some family resemblance somewhere.

My journey really began as a look at some of the interesting cultural and linguistic 'pearls' that are hidden in the Bible, particularly in that part Christianity calls the New Testament. The common term for the source of background information I had stumbled onto is 'the Hebraic roots' of the Scriptures. It opened up a veritable goldmine of insights and revelations into the meaning of the words and stories I thought I knew so well.

I had been a serious student of the Bible since I was a teenager. I had taught myself to get around quite well in the Greek text of the New Testament by the time I was nineteen years old. I have spent countless hundreds of hours reading and studying the Bible since then, but once I began to see and understand those words and stories from the Hebraic perspective the Bible became a whole new book for me. I felt as though I had spent twenty years getting to know what the Bible said, but now I was finding out what it *means*. It was like being given a decoder ring—the kind we used to get by sending in 50¢ and five cereal box-tops—so we could decipher the messages encrypted in the Sunday comics.

The first discovery I stumbled onto was realizing there is a reason the Bible makes so much more sense when viewed from a

Hebraic perspective: the Bible is a Jewish book written almost entirely by Jews from a Jewish perspective using Jewish style and figures of speech, and in most cases the recipients were also Jewish and/or familiar with Jewish culture. David Bivin and Roy Blizzard, Jr. explained it this way in their book *Understanding the Difficult Words of Jesus*:

> It should be emphasized that the Bible (both Old and New Testaments) is, in its entirety, highly Hebraic. In spite of the fact that portions of the New Testament were communicated in Greek, the background is thoroughly Hebrew. The writers are Hebrew, the culture is Hebrew, the religion is Hebrew, the traditions are Hebrew, and the concepts are Hebrew.[5]

We, in our western mindset, have been taught the interpretation of the Scriptures according to the 'early Church fathers;' Polycarp, Irenaeus, Chrysostom, Augustine, Origen and Jerome. But something is awry with this picture, as pointed out by John Shelby Spong:

> Western consciousness in this era [that of the Church fathers] was such that it escaped the notice of the common mind that all of the fathers of the Church were Gentiles of a Greek, Latin, or North African origin. It also did not occur to them to notice that the Gospels were books written by people who were Jewish...
> The fact that we must recover is that Christianity was not born as a Western religion. A Western mentality has been imposed on this Middle Eastern understanding or revelation of God. The Bible is a Jewish book. It was written by people who thought as Jews, embraced the world as Jews, and understood reality as Jews.

---

[5] David Bivin and Roy Blizzard Jr., *The Difficult Words of Jesus* (Shippensburg: Destiny Image 1994), p. 4

Indeed, one will never understand any of the gospels, I am convinced, unless and until one can embrace their essential Jewishness...For the truth found in the Gospels could be revealed only by reading these texts through a Jewish lens. That Jewish lens, however, remained hidden from Christian eyes for centuries.[6]

How did we get here from there?

As I delved into the past of Christianity, I discovered the cause that ultimately affected the reasons I am writing this book. Simply put, it is that the Church chose the path of anti-Semitism very early in its development and by doing so, disconnected itself from its roots or, to use a different analogy, slid off its foundation. In fact, it is only because of common understanding that I use the word 'church' to refer to Christianity since that is what it calls itself. In actuality, the word 'church' is our English form of the Scottish word *kirk*, which itself was borrowed from another language, and can be traced back to Circe (*SEER-say*), the ancient Roman goddess, said to be the daughter of the sun, who always had a circle of light around her head when she was pictured. Her worshippers always stood in a circle—in fact, we get the words 'circle,' 'circumference,' and circumnavigate' from her name.

The Greek word that most English Bibles render as 'church' is *ekklesia,* meaning 'the called out assembly.' Its Hebrew equivalent is *kehilah* which means 'congregation' or 'assembly.' When I was in Bible College, we were required to study Church history so we could learn from our forefathers of the faith. I didn't think anything of it at the time, but now as I peruse books on Church history I am struck by one glaring misconception: they all ascribe to the idea that the 'church' as we know it was born on the Day of Pentecost written about in the second chapter of the book of Acts. That is the commonly held position within Christianity—anti-Semitic Christianity, that is. "Why should I

---

[6] John Shelby Spong, *Liberating the Gospels; Reading the Bible with Jewish Eyes* (New York, Harper Collins 1996) p. 5, 18, 30, 35.

think otherwise?" you may ask. Because the called-out assembly had been around for centuries previous to the Acts 2 outpouring of the Holy Spirit.

The VERY early 'Church'

Christianity teaches that 'the called out assembly' refers to believers in Jesus who have been 'called out' of the world into a life of following the One who called them to "come unto Me." While that is a true statement as such, it is the subliminal message attached to it that taints the truth—that it was a new phenomenon on the earth that began that Pentecost, as described in Acts 2.

Around 200 BCE, 70 Hebrew scholars who were also fluent in Greek were commissioned to translate the Hebrew Scriptures (known in Christianity as the Old Testament) into Greek. This was necessary as a result of the military conquests of Alexander the Great that made Greek the common language of the known world. There were so many Jews around Africa, Europe and the Middle East who couldn't speak or read Hebrew that a translation was necessary in order for them to be able to learn their rich heritage. This translation became known as the *Septuagint*, meaning 'seventy' in Latin in honour of the scholars who did the work.[7]

In that translation, the Greek word they used repeatedly to describe the nation of Israel is *ekklesia*, and for good reason. It was the nation of Israel that was *called out* of Egypt at the time of the exodus. This truth was stated through the prophet Hosea when the LORD said,

When Israel was a child, I loved him,
And out of Egypt I called My son.[8]

Up until that point in time, the nation of Israel did not exist. When they had gone into Egypt, they were just a family of

---

[7] In theological works it is often abbreviated by the Roman numerals *LXX*.
[8] Hosea 11:1

seventy members.[9]   While in Egypt, they were an oppressed people without a leader or any type of government.   Their only unifying factor was their ancestry and their hatred of slavery.   But when they came out—when they were called out—they became 'the called out assembly;' *that* was the birthday of the 'church.'

It was the congregation of Israel who was led by God through the wilderness; to whom the oracles of God were entrusted; who eventually achieved their goal of the Promised Land; who vacillated between obedience and rebellion to the clear commands of God; who ended up being taken prisoner by their enemies for seventy years because of that rebellion.   Then, only a relatively few of whom returned to their homeland to once again try to live as God's model nation on earth; and to whom and for whom the Messiah came, and to whom was given the charge to be the light unto the Gentiles.

There is an example within the New Testament of *ekklesia* being used to refer to Israel.   In Acts 7 we have the account of Stephen's defence before the Sanhedrin[10] for the false charge of blasphemy.   In his defence, he gives a condensed summary of Israel's history in which he describes Moses as "*he who was with the* ekklesia *in the wilderness.*"[11]   You may say that Luke (the writer of Acts) and Stephen used that word because it described Israel at that time, but then the designation passes on to the followers of Jesus.   If so, then you are saying that God 'changed horses midstream.'   If we believe that God changed His mind about the nation of Israel, or that He only created and called them out for the purpose of being the physical channel through whom He would send Messiah, then there is a problem and it is this: if God could and would do that to Israel, the people to whose ancestor—Abraham—He gave an everlasting covenant, and to whom He made a multitude of promises of blessing, many of which were to come upon them in the 'last days,' then we have a covenant/promise-breaking God.   How then would we know that

---

[9] Deut.10:22

[10] The Jewish Supreme Court made up of seventy members plus the High Priest.

[11] It is worth noting that the translators of the King James Version translated *ekklesia* as 'church' in this instance, but none of the modern English versions do.

He wouldn't do the same thing again to us? Can we really believe him when He said, "I will never leave you or forsake you?" Perhaps He's changed His mind about returning to deliver His followers before He pours out His wrath upon the earth. It is inconsistent reasoning to believe that God would turn His back on one group but not the other. It is an affront to the character of God to believe that He has forsaken Israel and cast her aside because her purpose had been fulfilled.

Israel means Israel!

A common, albeit erroneous, solution to the Israel/Church controversy is to say that the Church has now replaced Israel in the plan of God; this is known as 'replacement theology.' This concept is not supported by a single verse of Scripture that I can find, but gets its support from centuries of anti-Semitism within Christianity that began in the second century CE. As I have shown that *'ekklesia'* is a reference to Israel, so I will show that 'Israel' also means Israel.

One can possibly understand that ancient theologians may have drawn their "the Church is now Israel" conclusion from the evidence that Israel as a nation virtually ceased to exist after the destruction of the temple in 70 CE took away their locus of worship, and then the Romans expelled all remaining Jews from 'Palestine'[12] after crushing the rebellion led by Simon Bar Kochba in 135 CE. But history shows that not all Bible scholars had written Israel out of existence forever. Men such as Sir Isaac Newton saw a resurrection of the nation of Israel in the last days predicted in detail through the writings of the prophets and even in the Pentateuch. It was only by refusal to spiritualise away the plain meaning of the text that they were able to foresee the rebirth of Israel. We, on the other hand, who live in this present time have no excuse for continuing to hold to this lie because Israel's existence cannot be denied.

---

[12] The name the Romans gave the land of Israel to provoke the Jews; it is the Latin form of 'Philistine.'

Throughout the *Torah* there are explicit indications that God always expected the Jews—and therefore Israel—to exist. One such example is found in Exodus 31:12-17 where God reiterates to Moses the importance of the Sabbath:

> [13] *"Speak also to the children of Israel, saying: 'Surely My Sabbaths you shall keep, for it is a sign between Me and you throughout your generations, that you may know that I am the LORD who sanctifies you...* [16] *Therefore the children of Israel shall keep the Sabbath, to observe the Sabbath throughout their generations as a **perpetual covenant.*** [17] *It is a sign between Me and the children of Israel **forever**."* (emphasis mine)

The words 'perpetual covenant' and 'forever' clearly imply continuance of the agreement. There is no hint of "Do this until..." within the context. He gave the Sabbath as a sign to Israel forever; we can conclude, then, that as long as Sabbath exists, then Israel, the people to whom it was given, will exist.[13]

Another example can be found in the instructions concerning the Feasts of the LORD outlined in Leviticus 23. The decree from God that "it shall be a statute forever throughout your generations" occurs four times in the chapter: in v. 14 relating to the Feast of Firstfruits; in v. 21 relating to the Feast of Weeks (Pentecost); in v. 31 relating to *Yom Kippur* (Day of Atonement); and in v. 41 relating to the Feast of Tabernacles. The same idea is conveyed in Ex. 12:13 about Passover. Again, nowhere in the text is the idea of 'until...' even implied.

Dozens of references can be found in the Prophets and the Psalms, which attest to the continuance of Israel as a people. One of the clearest and most emphatic is found in Jeremiah 31:35-37:

---

[13] Whether a person believes that Saturday or Sunday is the Sabbath is irrelevant to the point here. As long as there is a seven-day week, it is a testimony to God who created the world in six days and then rested on the seventh day. There is no logical explanation for a week of seven days.

Thus says the LORD, Who gives the sun for light by day,
The ordinances of the moon and the stars for a light by
night,
Who disturbs the sea, and its waves roar
(The LORD of Hosts is His name):
"If those ordinances depart from before Me, says the
LORD,
Then the seed of Israel shall also cease from being a
nation before Me forever."
Thus says the LORD:
"If heaven above can be measured,
And the foundations of the earth searched out beneath,
I will cast off all the seed of Israel for all that they have
done, says the LORD."

As long as the sun, moon, stars and sea continue in their place, then Israel—the Israel whom He led out of Egypt (see v.32)—will continue to exist before Almighty God. And until we can measure the universe and chart the depths of the earth, He will not cast away Israel for ALL they have done. That 'all' even includes breaking God's covenant, killing His prophets and rejecting His Messiah. They are His covenant people, the apple of His eye, His special treasure, His beloved; they have not been nor will they ever be forsaken.

In the New Testament,[14] the word 'Israel' appears 77 times, yet in not one single case can the word 'church' be inserted in its place and make sense. One may argue that Paul calls the church 'the Israel of God' in Galatians 6:16, but that meaning would have to be imposed upon the text since he doesn't explain who it is (a fact that supports the argument that 'Israel' means Israel), and the presence of the conjunction 'and' before it would set it off as separate from the previous group—"those who walk according to this rule," i.e., those who are already a new creation (v. 15).

---

[14] The term 'New Testament' itself is a derogatory anti-Semitic title coined by the early Gentile Church to indicate its supremacy over the 'old' Hebrew Scriptures.

Wouldn't that be a fitting description of the believers?[15]

What about the non-Jews?

After having said all that, we must reconstruct a proper theology for the relationship between Israel the *ekklesia* and the believing Gentiles. To do that we can go back to the time of the exodus from Egypt when the assembly was called out. Ex. 12:38 records that *"a mixed multitude went up with them also."* This refers to non-Israelites who were included in the great deliverance wrought by the hand of God for His people. We can deduce from the context that follows that verse that those non-Israelites must have also eaten the Passover the previous night. The provisions for that to have happened are listed in vs. 43-49; why else are they given at this time? Those who were not Israel in the flesh had to undergo circumcision—the sign of the covenant—before they could take part in the event. Notice the change in status that circumcision effects:

"...and he shall be as a native of the land." (v. 48)

In other words, "now consider him as one of you." Then in v. 49, God says,

"One law shall be for the native-born and for the stranger who dwells among you."

It is critical that we understand the full implications of what is stated here because only then can we see the truth that Yeshua and the apostles taught regarding the assembly. Simply put, it is this: when Gentiles come to faith in God and receive His salvation or deliverance provided through His Son—the true Passover sacrifice—then they are joined to Israel and are considered to be

---

[15] If so, then 'the Israel of God' would be unbelieving Israel. It must also be considered, as David Stern points out in his *Jewish New Testament Commentary* (p.572-574) that Paul was most likely adapting a common blessing from everyday Judaism known as the *Amidah* and using it as his benediction.

just as much the sons of Abraham.

Notice I said, "joined to Israel," not "displacing Israel." Paul said it clearly in Ephesians 2,

> *[11] You, once Gentiles in the flesh…*
> *[12] …were without Messiah, being aliens from the commonwealth of Israel and strangers from the covenants of promise, having no hope and without God in the world.*

Pretty bleak description of where they came from. But notice that it is past tense! If we have believed the gospel, then that description no longer applies. The good news is

> *[13] But now in Messiah Yeshua, you who were once far off have been brought near by the blood of Messiah.*
> *[19] Now, therefore, you are no longer strangers and foreigners, but fellow citizens with the saints and members of the household of God…*

We are included into them! We are now part of the commonwealth of Israel, included in the covenants of promise and fellow-citizens. That sounds like a national identity to me.

In Romans 11, Paul illustrated this joining by saying that the Gentiles have been grafted into the olive tree. Paul got that analogy from Jeremiah 11:16 where the olive tree is plainly depicted as a euphemism for Israel. The context is set in verse 2 of Jeremiah 11 when God tells Jeremiah to "*speak to the men of Judah and the inhabitants of Jerusalem*" the following, which we pick up in verse 16,

> *The LORD called your name,*
> *Green Olive Tree, Lovely and of Good Fruit.*
> *With the noise of a great tumult*
> *He has kindled fire on it,*
> *And its branches are broken.*

Had the early Gentile believers been willing to see this truth, the entire course of history would have been changed. Instead of persecuting the Jews, they would have protected them as their own flesh and blood. Christianity owes everything to the Jews; they copied and protected the Word of God for centuries at immense cost; they stood faithful through attempted genocide and survived to '*give birth to a Male Child who was caught up to God and His throne and who will rule all nations with a rod of iron;* '[16] they were 'sacrificed' by God so that salvation could come to the Gentiles,[17] and it is only our identification with them that qualifies us to enter the kingdom.[18]

What about the New Covenant?

Even the basis for the 'New Testament' is evidence against this separatist or replacement attitude of the Church. When Yeshua raised the cup that night during His last Passover supper with His disciples and said, "This cup is the new covenant in My blood," they instantly knew what He meant (although admittedly it did take awhile for it to sink in).

In the *Torah*, God made it clear that every covenant must be confirmed or ratified with blood.[19] It was so in the case with Noah,[20] Abraham,[21] and with Moses and the Israelites at Sinai.[22] Even the pronouncement of the 'new covenant' was not a foreign concept to their thinking. It had been foretold long before that

---

[16] Rev.12:5

[17] Had Israel not been blinded to Messiah (Rom. 11:25) but received Him, it would have ushered in the Messianic Kingdom and the judgment on the nations. It would have been 'game over' for Gentiles. Instead, their being blinded left the Jewish people vulnerable to the atrocities of the inquisitions, pogroms, expulsions, crusades and the Holocaust perpetrated by those same Gentiles. Many Christians will stand in horror on the Day of Judgment when the Son of Man says, "In as much as you did it to the least of these My brethren, you did it to Me."

[18] The twelve gates to the New Jerusalem are designated for the twelve tribes of Israel. (Rev.21:12)

[19] See Heb. 9:18

[20] Gen. 8:20

[21] Gen. 15:9-10

[22] Ex. 24:8

night, and Israel had been awaiting its arrival.

I have spoken with many Christians in the last few years who firmly state that they are 'new covenant believers,' or that they belong to a 'new covenant church.' I wonder to myself if they are really aware of the Scriptural definition of the new covenant and who and what it involves. When I ask the question to that effect, my suspicions that they have no idea of the new covenant's prediction are validated.

It is found in the book of Jeremiah, chapter 31. The context of this prophecy is when Nebuchadnezzar and his Babylonian army had surrounded and besieged Jerusalem. The inhabitants of the city were terrified and waiting nervously for their attackers to burst through the walls and destroy the city and the Temple. Jeremiah was in Jerusalem at the time and, in fact, had warned of just such a judgment on the nation. Yet, in the deep despair of those days, God gave Jeremiah a message of hope for the people:

> *"Behold, the days are coming, says the LORD, when I will make a new covenant with the house of Israel and the house of Judah—not according to the covenant that I made with their fathers in the day that I took them by the hand to lead them out of Egypt, My covenant which they broke, though I was a husband to them, says the LORD. But this is the covenant that I will make with the house of Israel after those days, says the LORD: I will put My law in their minds, and write it on their hearts; and I will be their God, and they shall be My people. No more shall every man teach his neighbour, and every man his brother, saying, 'Know the LORD,' for they shall all know Me, from the least of them to the greatest of them, says the LORD. For I will forgive their iniquity, and their sin I will remember no more."[23]*

---

[23] Jer. 31:31-34

God acknowledged they had broken His covenant and was ready to punish them for their rebellion,[24] but He lifted their eyes to the future when they will be restored to Him and His ways. There are several key issues in these few verses, which will give us a correct understanding of what this is all about.

First, we must consider the word 'new.' Though in Hebrew it conveys the idea of 'new,' the same word is also used by Jeremiah in Lamentations 3:23 where he describes God's mercies and compassion as *"new every morning."* Ps. 100:5 (among others) tells us that His mercy is everlasting, so it is not that God creates a fresh batch of mercy each morning, but that He gives it back to us afresh each new day. Also, this word is from the same root as the word translated as 'month' or 'new moon' but actually means 'renewal.' The Hebrew phrase *Rosh Chodesh,* translated as 'new moon,' literally means 'head of the renewal.' It is not that a brand new moon is created each month,[25] but that the moon is renewed for another cycle.

Second, tying into the theme of this chapter is the explicit stipulation regarding who will be the parties included in this 'new' covenant: God, the house of Israel and the house of Judah. Period. If anyone who is not of the houses of Israel or Judah[26] wants to enter this covenant, they must first join themselves to one of these houses. Whether you call it being grafted in or some other term is irrelevant, but one thing for certain is that replacement is not an option. Along this same line is a statement from Yeshua's own mouth recorded in Matthew 15:24,

---

[24] According to Jeremiah 25:11-12 and 29:10, he knew that Judah would be disciplined for 70 years but doesn't appear to know why it was to be that long. We are told in 2 Chr. 36:21 that the 70 years were due to Israel not having given the land its Sabbath-year rest for the previous 490 years. Thus, Israel owed the land 70 years of rest and God was using Nebuchadnezzar as His collection agent.

[25] The English word 'month' is derived from the word 'moon,' although we don't consider a month to be the length of a lunar cycle as the Jews do.

[26] The words 'house of Israel and house of Judah' refer to the two kingdoms into which the whole nation of Israel split after Solomon's death.

"I was not sent except to the lost sheep of the house of Israel."

If I were a betting man, I'd wager that that verse doesn't get much 'air time' from the average Christian pulpit.

And third, it must be realized just what the terms and conditions are that make up this 'new covenant.' There are some who argue over the exact meaning of this Hebrew word translated as 'new,' as to whether it means 'new' or 'renewed.' If I based my entire claim on the meaning of a single word, then my case would be very weak. However, the text leaves no room for doubt about whether this 'new covenant' is a completely different agreement or a re-communication of the former one when it says,

"This is the covenant...I will put my law (Heb. Torah) *in their minds and write it on their hearts."*

He is trying, at least, to put the *Torah* in the hearts of His new covenant people. That's how the first century believers understood it, evidenced by the fact that the writer of the book of Hebrews quoted this section from Jeremiah not once, but twice.[27] The content of the covenant is not being changed, just how it is being communicated; so the notion that what Yeshua came to bring us is a completely different covenant is totally false.

This portion in Jeremiah is the only place in the entire Old Testament that a 'new covenant' is mentioned and, therefore, would have been the first and only point of reference for the disciples. It is our only reference point as well; it establishes the foundation upon which we can build. To be a new covenant believer is to be a living scroll for the pen of a ready writer. Or, as Paul aptly capsulized the transition to the new covenant,

"Clearly you are an epistle of Messiah, ministered by us, written not with ink but by the Spirit of the living God, not on

---

[27] Heb. 8:8-12; 10:16-17

tablets of stone but on tablets of flesh, that is, of the heart. "[28]

It is noteworthy that he matter-of-factly implies that what is written will be the same—only the medium for its imprint will be changed.

The foreigners who join

Yet another unmistakeable reference to the expectation that the Gentiles who desire to live in a covenant relationship with God will also live as and consider themselves a part of Israel can be found in Isaiah 56. In my Bible there is a chapter heading that says 'Salvation for the Gentiles.' The first eight verses of the chapter are a message from the LORD to these Gentiles:

> *Thus says the LORD:*
> *"Keep justice and do righteousness, for My salvation is about to come, and My righteousness to be revealed.*
> *Blessed is the man who does this, and the son of man who lays hold on it; who keeps from defiling the Sabbath, and keeps his hand from doing any evil.*
> *Do not let the son of the foreigner who has joined himself to the LORD speak, saying,*
> *"The LORD has utterly separated me from His people;"*
> *nor let the eunuch say, "Here I am, a dry tree."*
> *For thus says the LORD:*
> *To the eunuchs who keep My Sabbaths, and choose what pleases Me, and hold fast My covenant, even to them I will give in My house and within My walls a place and a name better than that of sons and daughters;*
> *I will give them an everlasting name that shall not be cut off.*
>
> *"Also the sons of the foreigner who join themselves to the*

---

[28] 2 Cor. 3:3

> LORD, *to serve Him, and to love the name of the* LORD, *to be His servants—everyone who keeps from defiling the Sabbath, and holds fast My covenant—even them I will bring to My holy mountain, and make them joyful in My house of prayer.*
> *"Their burnt offerings and their sacrifices will be accepted on My altar; for My house shall be called a house of prayer for all nations."*
> *The* LORD *God who gathers the outcasts of Israel, says,*
> *"Yet I will gather to him others besides those who are gathered to him."*

For the present time I will delay commenting on verses 1 and 2 since they more explicitly deal with righteousness and the Sabbath, topics to be discussed in other chapters.

Verse 3 contains some words pertinent to the topic at hand; the LORD is speaking to 'foreigners' who have joined themselves to Him, and He forbids them to say, *"The* LORD *has utterly separated me from His people."* At first reading, the connotation of that forbidden remark is that the foreigners, i.e., those who aren't of Israel, are prone to feeling inferior to God's chosen people—so much so that they feel excluded from His family. God wants to make sure that Gentiles know they are accepted as equals with Israelites (see vs. 5 & 7).

But there is also an alternate meaning that can be derived from verse 3, one that Gentile believers, for the most part, have missed. It is that they should not say that God has made them a separate entity from Israel and that He has a different plan for them, or will deal with them differently. If we take the inverse approach to this verse and put it into the positive sense, it says, *"Let the son of the foreigner...say, The* LORD *has utterly joined me to His people.'"*

Either way you choose to look at this verse, the truth is plain that believing Gentiles are to consider themselves as part of Israel. The conclusion is stated in verse 8 that the LORD God will gather *others* to him, i.e., to Israel. This concept is repeated by Yeshua in John 10 where He claims to be the Good Shepherd.[29] In John 10:16 He says,

> *"And other sheep I have which are not of this fold; them also I must bring, and they will hear My voice; and there will be one flock and one shepherd."*

There isn't a Bible scholar I know of who interprets the phrase 'other sheep' to be anything other than Gentiles. If that is the correct understanding (and I believe it is), then according to Yeshua's own words there will only be **one** flock, made up of Jews and Gentiles.

Let's go back to Romans 11 for one last example that expresses the expectation of Gentiles to be gathered to and included in Israel. After giving the analogy of Gentiles being grafted in (vs. 16-24), Paul explains in verses 25-26 that blindness has been imposed upon Israel "until the fullness of the Gentiles has come in. And so all Israel will be saved." The two key words in this section are 'in' and 'all.' 'In' expresses Paul's position that the Gentiles will be added to Israel. 'All' expresses his belief that there are some who are of Israel who are not Israel, i.e., they aren't of physical descent from Jacob. God, by His foreknowledge, knows who they are and is grafting them in.

Who is "My brother"?

It is detestable to look at history and see the evil perpetrated upon the Jews by the Christian Church 'in the name of Jesus.' The separation between them was man's response to worldly persecution; it was never intended to happen by the LORD in whose name they claimed to have made the breach and then inflicted retribution. It has been said that he who claims to be a Christian and hates the Jews is not really a follower of Christ. I

---

[29] This claim to be the Good Shepherd is no less than a claim to be the one who spoke through Ezekiel in 34:11 where the LORD declares, "I, Myself, will search for My sheep and search them out." To which sheep is He referring? The lost sheep of the house of Israel (see Ezk. 34:1, 29-30).

would take it one step further and say that even an apathetic attitude towards them belies an unregenerate heart.

Yeshua gave us a picture of what Judgment Day—that day when all will stand before Him and give account for our deeds while on earth—will be like. It is again the passage in Matt. 25:31-46. The nations will be gathered before Him to determine their final destination. There is only one single criterion for judgment: "How did you treat My brethren?"

Christianity has fostered the myth that those 'brethren' to whom He is referring are the downtrodden of society, the unfortunate, the helpless; there is an element of truth to that. We are admonished to care for the poor, the widows and the fatherless. But the greater truth is seen when we understand that references to 'the nations' in the Bible mean all those other than Israel. In Hebrew, the word is *goyim*, not necessarily a derogatory term, but one which distinguishes that they are not Israelites. The Greek word used to convey the same idea is *ethne,* from which we get the English word 'ethnic' to describe people groups. We also see from Balaam's first prophecy over Israel that it is "a people dwelling alone, not reckoning itself among the nations."[30] Israel is never considered to be just another one of the nations—it is set apart.

The Feast of the Nations

At the yearly celebration of the Feast of Tabernacles or Booths, Israel would sacrifice a total of seventy bulls over a seven-day period as burnt offerings for the other nations of the world.[31] Then on the eighth day they would offer one bull as a

---

[30] Num. 23:9

[31] The Hebraic reckoning of there being seventy nations throughout the earth is derived from Dt. 32:8,

> *"When the Most High divided their* [Israel's] *inheritance to the nations* [Heb. goyim], *when He separated the sons of Adam, He set the boundaries of the peoples according to the number of the children of Israel."*

Genesis 46:27 states that there were seventy people who were of the house of Jacob (Israel) when they went into Egypt. They were said to have 'come from his body' (v.26), i.e., they were considered 'his children.' The seventy who went into

burnt offering for themselves. As God's chosen representatives on earth, they were to keep themselves separated unto Him, not only socially, but symbolically as well. In similar fashion, the Sanhedrin was composed of seventy-one members; one to represent (symbolically) each nation, plus the High Priest to represent Israel. With this as the cultural understanding then, the 'nations' assembled before the Son of Man are those which are non-Israelite, and "My brethren" are the Jews and those who have joined themselves to Israel.

Truth or consequences

I realize that it may come as a shock to you when I put it in such black-and-white terms. You may be slightly (or more) offended by my telling you that you might possibly be on the receiving end of the interrogation from the Son of Man on that Day. It was not my intention to bring offence, but to acquaint you with a Scripturally-based, non-anti-Semitic perspective of those verses.

The Church has misappropriated many prophecies and promises that belong to physical Israel, with the result being devastating consequences to both: the Church languishes in self-deception and false security; Israel has entrenched itself against the Church and, sadly, their own Messiah—whom the Church claims taught them to hate or ignore the Jews. It is only by seeing and acknowledging Israel's true position in the plan of God that believers—Jew or Gentile—can find their own place in the body.

Both Christianity and Judaism look forward to the day when Messiah will appear and bring the rule of man on earth to its appointed end and establish His kingdom of righteousness. There are a few cataclysmic events set to take place on a global scale before that kingdom is set up. Prior to those events, we all expect one great happening: the angel who spoke to Daniel described it like this,

---

Egypt are seen as typifying the nations of the world who went into bondage to sin and need a deliverer to bring them out.

Also, in Gen. 10 are listed seventy nations, which descended from Noah and his sons.

> *"At that time **your people** shall be delivered,*
> *Everyone who is found written in the book.*
> *And many of those who sleep in the dust of the earth shall*
>   *awake,*
> *Some to everlasting life,*
> *Some to everlasting shame and contempt."*[32]

Zechariah prophesied,

> *"The* LORD *will be seen over **them**,* [the daughter of Zion, v. 9]
> *And His arrow will go forth like lightning.*
> *The* LORD *God will blow the trumpet,*
> *And go with whirlwinds from the south...*
> *The* LORD *their God will save **them** in that day,*
> *As **the flock of His people**,*
> *For **they** shall be like the jewels of a crown,*
> *Lifted like a banner over His land.*[33]

Paul described it this way:

> *"The* LORD *Himself will descend from heaven with a shout, with the voice of an archangel, and with the trumpet of God. And the dead in Messiah will rise first. Then we who are alive and remain shall be caught up together with them in the clouds to meet the* LORD *in the air."*[34]

In Matt. 24:31, Yeshua Himself told us:

> *"He will send His angels with a great sound of a trumpet, and they will gather together His elect from the four winds, from one end of heaven to the other."*

---

[32] Dan. 12:1c-2
[33] Zech. 9:14,16
[34] 1 Thess. 4:16-17

All these are descriptions of what we call the resurrection and rapture. What an awesome day that will be! There is, however, one very important detail we cannot ignore. Who is being referred to as the ones who will be 'delivered,' 'saved,' 'caught up,' or 'gathered together from the four winds?' The angel told Daniel it would be 'your people;' Zechariah said it would be Judah and Ephraim; Yeshua said it would be 'His elect.'[35]

Either in or out

No matter where we turn in the Bible, the inescapable truth is that God's plan of redemption and deliverance **only includes Israel.** The invitation has been extended to all who desire to 'come in,' become 'fellow citizens' and become 'members of the household of God.' Those who disregard that invitation as irrelevant or despise it as undesirable may one day see the folly of their choice—too late. My prayer is that you will choose to enter while the door is still open.

---

[35] Is. 45:4 clearly defines the elect of God as Israel.

Chapter 3
From Sabbath to Sunday

Without question, the first major hurdle that confronts anyone who investigates Messianic Judaism is the Sabbath. Which day is it? Does it really make a difference? Isn't every day a Sabbath-rest now? All these questions and more presented themselves to me in the course of my search; I had to answer each one before making my decision because it is a foundational issue within Christianity. In discussions with Christians over the last few years, nothing has evoked such heated and defensive reactions like broaching the topic of the Sabbath. Even when presented with evidence that contradicts their position, they cling tenaciously to what they have been taught.

What is it about the issue of Sabbath that elicits such a response? I recall a discussion at a meeting of the executive board of our local ministerial association while I was still a pastor. We were brainstorming about ways to increase attendance at the monthly pastors' gatherings as well as facilitate healthier connections between churches. My own church was renting our facility to two other church groups at the time; one group rented from us on Sunday afternoon, the other—Seventh Day Adventists—rented on Saturday. I had noticed that none of the Seventh Day Adventist pastors ever attended the ministerial meetings, so I suggested to the executive board that we extend an invitation to them. The president informed me in no uncertain terms that he would resign immediately should the rest of the board vote in favour of inviting them! He said he personally would have had no problem with doing it, but during a previous tenure as president of the ministerial, he had received hate mail (those were his words) from other pastors in town for allowing some Seventh Day Adventist pastors to attend the meetings.

The Seventh Day Adventists are a group that adheres to the basic fundamental teachings of Christianity and was declared **not** to be a cult by Dr. Walter Martin in his classic reference work *The Kingdom of the Cults*. What causes such an unwarranted bias against them from [other] Christians? Sabbath. The Seventh Day Adventists claim it is Saturday, the seventh day of the week, and it flies in the face of mainline Christianity.

When I was first confronted with the question of why Christianity regards Sunday as the Sabbath, I simply repeated the reasoning and justifications I had been taught over the years. I had accepted those reasons unquestioningly because they seemed to make sense and, more importantly, they came from what I deemed to be an authoritative source. The question motivated me to investigate this 'Sabbath issue,' but I was confident that my findings would verify my stance on the subject. To my surprise, the more digging I did to discover the truth, the more I undermined my own position.

Christianity's 'pat answers'

The 'pat answers' of Christianity to the Sabbath question generally fall into three groups:

1. Christians worship on Sunday—the first day of the week—because it commemorates Jesus' resurrection on Sunday morning.
2. That the commandment to honour the Sabbath day is the only one of the Ten Commandments that Jesus didn't restate, update and validate during His ministry, thereby indicating that it was not significant for the New Covenant era.
3. That now, in this New Covenant era, we have ceased our working to earn God's approval by obeying a set of restrictive laws and have entered into the true rest of which the Sabbath was just a foreshadow. Now every day is a Sabbath for us to enjoy.

There are some well-documented books that deal with this topic in detail, such as *From Sabbath to Sunday* by Dr. Samuelle Bacciocci, and *Too Long In the Sun* by Richard M. Rives, which may be obtained if a more technical understanding of the change is desired. For my purpose in this book, I will condense some of the information gathered from many sources, as well as present some of my own arguments, to expose the error beneath the three pat answers.

1. Sunday morning (first day of the week) resurrection

That the resurrection took place early 'on the first day of the week' is plainly stated in the gospels.[1] Or is it? What is plainly stated is that Yeshua had risen before the women arrived at the tomb 'early on the first day of the week.'[2] In fact, Matthew records that He had risen and was gone *before* the stone was rolled away. So just when did the resurrection happen?

To answer that, we have to take a look at the original languages, i.e., the Greek copies of the gospels and the Hebrew spoken by Jews at that time. The words 'on the first day of the week' are a poor and very biased translation of the Greek words *mian ton Sabbaton.* If you look up the words in a Greek lexicon, you will find that neither 'day' nor 'week' is really in the text. The Greek word for 'day' is *hemera* and the word for 'week' is listed as *Sabbaton,* but that meaning is imposed on the word. You may have noticed that the word *Sabbaton* bears a striking resemblance to the word 'Sabbath.' How did it get translated as 'week?'

In Hebrew, the word for Sabbath is *Shabbat;* the word for seven is *shavua,* and it is also the word for 'week.' The Greek word *Sabbaton* is merely a transliteration from the Hebrew word *Shabbat,*[3] which always means Sabbath. So when the translators were confronted with *mian ton Sabbaton* (which literally means 'first of the Sabbath'), it didn't make sense to them so they turned *Shabbat* into *shavua;* 'Sabbath' into 'seven' or 'week.'

---

[1] Mat. 28:1-6; Mark 16:1-6; Luke 24:1-6; John 20:1-7

[2] This is the reason given for Easter morning sunrise services. Actually, neither Easter nor sunrise has anything to do with the resurrection. See chapter 5 for more information about the origins of 'Easter.'

[3] In Greek, there is no 'sh' sound, so 's' was as close as they could get.

W.E. Vine explains it this way:
Sabbaton is used in the plural in the phrase 'the first day of the week.'[4]
Yet under the entry 'Sabbath' he says:
Sabbaton or *Sabata*: the latter, the plural form, was transliterated from the Aramaic word that was mistaken for a plural; **hence the singular, *sabbaton*, was formed from it**.[5] (emphasis mine)
So *Sabbaton* means Sabbath—singular.

But when viewed from a Hebraic perspective, a different picture emerges. If *mian ton Sabbaton* is translated into Hebrew[6] it becomes *echad b'shabbat*— 'first of the Sabbath,' an idiomatic expression used to describe the first three stars that appear on the Sabbath which signal that it has ended.[7] Mary and the other women could not have gone to the tomb on the Sabbath because that would have been a violation of the Sabbath. Therefore, they waited for the Sabbath to be over and went as soon as they could. So, rather than provide evidence for a Sunday morning resurrection, when understood Hebraically it points to a resurrection time of late afternoon/early evening on Saturday. Although Messiah probably 'rested' in the grave on the Sabbath and rose soon after sunset—and Hebraically that is the first day of the week—it still is not Sunday morning.

The calendar we observe today is of Roman origin, with days beginning and ending at midnight. God's way of reckoning days is from sunset to sunset. Thus, when the early congregations met on the 'first day of the week,' it was Saturday evening on today's calendar. Their practice was to attend synagogue on Sabbath

---

[4] *Vine's Expository Dictionary of New Testament Words*, p. 1229 – 'week.'
[5] Ibid. p. 993
[6] Dr. James Trimm has presented weighty evidence, including this simple example, in a hypothesis which states that much, if not all, of the New Testament was originally written in Hebrew and later translated into Greek. (See his introduction to the *Hebraic-Roots Version "New Testament,"* translated by James S. Trimm; published by the Society for the Advancement of Nazarene Judaism, Hurst TX, 2001.)
[7] On the Hebrew calendar, a day begins at sunset and ends the following sunset.

morning with their fellow Jews, then gather for *Havdollah*[8] around sunset and continue with fellowship, teaching and preaching into the evening. The story in Acts 20 of Eutychus getting sleepy and falling from the window to the street below because Paul preached until midnight and beyond was the result of a gathering that had begun early (at sunset) 'on the first day of the week,' not sometime early Sunday morning.

Another cultural hindrance we have in comprehending this Sabbath/Sunday issue is that we in the Western society of the 21st century are accustomed to a two-day weekend. This was not the case in first-century Israel. The Romans had shown religious tolerance to the Jews and allowed them to retain their Sabbath day, and the Jews followed the fourth commandment as it was written: "Six days shall you labour and do all your work."[9] Their 'weekend' consisted of Sabbath, period. The first day of the week—Sunday as we know it—was a day of labour and business.

A further weakness to pat answer number one is that it is based on a practice mentioned only in 1 Corinthians 16:2 where Paul says,

"When you come together on the first day of the week..."

The context of this verse is referring to an offering that the congregation in Corinth would be sending with him to the believers in Israel who were in the middle of a famine at the time. Paul tells them to collect the offering on the 'first day of the week' so it would be ready when he passed through on his way to Jerusalem. The reason they were to collect it then was that Jewish tradition, based on certain passages in the book of Nehemiah, forbade them from handling money for any reason on the Sabbath.

But whatever the reason, for Paul's instruction, the context doesn't contain any kind of directive that says, "Do not have your assembly on the Sabbath as the Jews do, but come together on the day after, like all the Christian churches do." He just makes the

---

[8] Hebrew for 'separation,' a simple ceremony of closing the Sabbath.
[9] Ex. 20:9

comment in passing, *"When you come together."* We could just as easily say that Paul mentioned the 'first day of the week' to the Corinthians because they were the only congregation that met on that day. Perhaps the group in Philippi met on the third day and those in Colosse met on the sixth day. Acts 2:46-47 seems to imply that the congregation in Jerusalem gathered on a daily basis. That is equally as authoritative as the verse in 1 Corinthians 16. Also in the context in Acts 2 is the fact that everyone pooled their money and possessions together so the whole congregation could use them. Why isn't that principle followed?

The truth is that nowhere in the New Testament can a clear directive for changing the Sabbath to Sunday be found. So how and when did it happen? We'll look at that after we examine pat answers number 2 and 3. But this point, i.e., a lack of clear directive, is, in a sense, the flip-side of pat answer number 2:

2. Sabbath is not validated in the New Testament

The basis of this argument rests on the claim that Yeshua bypassed the Sabbath commandment in His teaching and thereby indicated that it had been abrogated. Again, we have a conclusion based on non-evidence, but we will ignore that for the present and confront the statement.

First of all, the Sabbath commandment isn't the only one of the Ten Commandments not endorsed verbally by Yeshua or His disciples. When I am rebuffed in a Sabbath discussion with pat answer number 2, I offer the person $50 if they can show me where the third commandment—that of not taking the name of the LORD in vain—is restated in the New Testament. No one has found even a hint of it yet. But who in Christianity would dare say that profaning the name of God is now alright to do?

Although there appears to be no direct spoken instruction regarding the Sabbath, we can find many instances where both Yeshua and His followers did, in fact, keep the Sabbath. For example, in Luke 4:16ff we have the account of Yeshua returning to Nazareth. In verse 16, Luke wrote,

" ...and as His custom was, He went into the synagogue on the Sabbath day."

Part of the commandment of observing the Sabbath day is to have a 'holy convocation,'[10] i.e., a gathering for the specific purpose of honouring God by setting the day apart from the other six days. Yeshua was being obedient to the instructions for the Sabbath. We find a similar remark from Luke about Paul in Acts 17:2, that his custom was to go to the synagogue on the Sabbath.

In Mark 2 we can overhear a confrontation between Yeshua and some Pharisees concerning what can or cannot be done on the Sabbath. (For the record, I would like to bring attention to the fact that the *validity* of the Sabbath is not in question, just its proper *observance*.) In this account, Yeshua makes two statements that have great significance to our topic.

The first is found in verse 27, where Yeshua states that *"The Sabbath was made for man, not man for the Sabbath."* The Sabbath is a gift from God to His creation. Violation of the day by failing to honour it is a direct reflection of a person's attitude towards Him who gave it. It was given as a respite from the rat race, a retreat from the daily grind. The Jews refer to it as 'a cathedral in time.' How many cases of 'burnout' and being 'stressed out' could have been avoided by accepting this wonderful gift? Probably most of them. Notice, also, that Yeshua said it was made for *man*—not just for the Jews.

It is another perversion of truth within Christianity to believe and teach that the institution and observance of the Sabbath was solely for Israel and not the other nations of the world. As I pointed out previously, the understanding was that when people from the nations came to faith in the God of Abraham, Isaac and Jacob, they would join themselves to Israel and be considered as one who was native-born.

In Isaiah 56 there is an unmistakeable connection implied between the Sabbath and anyone who would have a relationship

---

[10] Lev. 23:3

with the LORD.

> *"Blessed is he who does this, and the son of man who lays hold on it;*
> *Who keeps from defiling the Sabbath and keeps his hand from doing any evil...*
> ***Also the sons of the foreigner*** *who join themselves to the* LORD *to serve Him, and to love the name of the* LORD, *to be His servants—**everyone who keeps from defiling the Sabbath** and holds fast My covenant—even them I will bring to My holy mountain and make them joyful in My house of prayer.*
> *Their burnt offerings and their sacrifices will be accepted on My altar;*
> *For My house will be called a house of prayer for **all nations**."*[11] (emphasis mine)

The words 'foreigner' and 'all nations' which bracket verses 6-7 leave no doubt about the all-inclusiveness of the promise: those who will be brought to His holy mountain are those who keep from defiling the Sabbath and hold fast His covenant. The latter are also the definition of being a servant of the LORD in this context.

The second significant statement found in Mark 2 is in verse 28. Yeshua said He is *Lord of the Sabbath.* He never claimed to be Lord of any other day. Yes, He is Lord of every day, but he made a point of emphasizing His connection to the Sabbath.

In the book of Hebrews, I found what I believe to be a clear directive for us about Sabbath.

> *"There remains, therefore, a rest for the people of God."*[12]

All through this fourth chapter the author has spoken of God's rest, which lies ahead for us to enter. In each case, he uses the

---

[11] Isaiah 56:2, 6-7
[12] Heb. 4:9

Greek word *katapausis* which simply means 'rest.' Thayer's Greek Lexicon adds:

> Metaphorically, the heavenly blessedness in which God dwells, and of which He has promised to make persevering believers in Christ partakers after the toils and trials of life on earth are ended.[13]

However, in verse 9, quoted above, the writer uses the Greek word *Sabbatismos*, which means 'to keep the Sabbath.'[14] The word 'remains' is better translated 'is left behind.'[15] So this verse should read:

> *"There is left behind, therefore, a Sabbath-keeping for the people of God."*

Why is Sabbath-keeping left for us to do? Because not only is it a weekly reminder of God's act of creating the world and His resting afterward, but it is a weekly taste of what is waiting for us when we are taken to be with Him—that 'heavenly blessedness.'

It is impossible to explain or describe the blessings that come from resting on the Sabbath day. Christians have been fed the lie that keeping Sabbath is legalism and bondage; nothing could be further from the truth! When one receives it as a gift from a loving heavenly Father, a day where one doesn't work—not because one can't, but because one doesn't have to; a day for which God says He will provide for our needs—then it truly is a day of rest: physically, emotionally and spiritually. (Incidentally, I've never been able to figure out why keeping Sabbath on Saturday is considered being legalistic but keeping it on Sunday is being 'under grace.')

---

[13] *Thayer's Greek-English Lexicon of the New Testament;* Zondervan Publishing House, 1975, p. 335
[14] ibid. p. 565
[15] So also in verses 1 and 6

3. Now every day is a Sabbath

Pat answer number three appeared recently in one of our local newspapers. There is a weekly column called 'Life Questions' in which a selected question from a reader is answered by a member of the ministerial association. That particular week, a question about the Sabbath was mailed in and the clergyman expounded for several paragraphs before stating his conclusion that now each and every day is a Sabbath to believers in Jesus. But let's examine this conclusion against the word of God.

To begin with, after six days of creative activity—called 'the first day...the second day...etc.'—God rested on the seventh day. After each of the first six days, it is recorded that 'God saw that it (i.e., whatever He had created that day) was good.' After the sixth day, the verdict from God was that everything He had made was *very* good. However, the description of the seventh day is a different theme altogether:

"Then God blessed the seventh day and sanctified it."[16]

Right from the time of creation, the seventh day has been distinct from all the other days. The very fact that we still regulate our schedules according to a seven-day week is a powerful testimony to the One who created the universe. Truthfully, it is nothing short of a miracle that the seven-day week continues to be observed; every other time-related institution that God set up has been corrupted and destroyed by man:

- Days are no longer counted from sundown to sundown, but from midnight to midnight;
- Months are no longer determined by the new moon (even though the word 'month' comes from 'moon'), but by people who set out to divide the year more evenly;

---

[16] Gen. 2:3

- Years are no longer determined by a cycle of twelve new moons (with an extra month added occasionally to keep Passover in the spring), but by the revolution of the earth around the sun.

It is little wonder that Christianity is in confusion about the 'end times'—God is still using His calendar and they are using the world's.

Why is a seven-day week still around in the 21st century? Not because it fits well with months or years. It still exists because it is God's stamp on creation, just like a craftsman who puts his mark on his handiwork. Which day is the seventh day? A quick glance at a calendar will answer that. Which day is the Sabbath day? The day we call Saturday, the same day which, incidentally, is known as *Sabado* in Spanish.

The Fourth Commandment

Remember the Sabbath day to keep it holy. [17]

I would like to highlight some important words of this commandment, which are often overlooked or misunderstood. The first is 'remember.' This doesn't simply imply an exercise of the mind but an experience of our whole being; we are to remember that it is a gift from God. The Sabbath was actually given to Israel and commanded by God before they reached Mt. Sinai. Israel had been travelling for a month and they were starting to get hungry. The LORD began providing manna for them, but in that provision was also a test for them:

> Then the LORD said to Moses, "Behold, I will rain bread from heaven for you. And the people shall go out and gather a certain quota every day, **that I may test them,** whether they will walk in my law [Heb. Torah] or not. And it shall be on the sixth day that they shall prepare what they bring in, and it shall be twice as much as they

---

[17] Ex. 20:8

gather daily. "[18] (emphasis mine)

What was the test? Whether the people would trust Him to provide enough for the seventh day without them having to go and gather it. Moses instructed the people on the sixth day,

> *"This is what the LORD has said: 'Tomorrow is a Sabbath rest, a holy Sabbath to the LORD. Bake what you will bake today and boil what you will boil; and lay up for yourselves all that remains, to be kept until morning.' "[19]*

Then on the seventh day he said,

> *"Eat that today, for today is a Sabbath to the LORD; today you will not find it in the field. Six days you shall gather it, but on the seventh day, the Sabbath, there will be none."[20]*

The way we remember the Sabbath day is by resting from our regular work. We are to trust God that He has provided enough for us in six days to sustain us for the seventh day. We don't go out and try to provide for ourselves; it is His promise to take care of us that day. It is His gift of a day off, a 'weekly holiday' if you will.

The second important word is 'the.' The word 'the' is defined as a definite article, used when one wants to denote a specific item or thing. *The* Sabbath day has a completely different connotation than *a* Sabbath day. When pressed on the issue of Sabbath, Christians will also revert to a variation of pat answer number three and say they recognize the need for a day of rest each week, but it can be any day, not just Saturday. Many people have to work shift work or in the retail industry, and taking Saturdays off is not an option, so they rationalize their Sabbath to be Monday or

---

[18] Ex. 16:4-5
[19] Ex. 16:23
[20] Ex. 16:25-26

some other day of the week. While this is an improvement over no day of rest, it falls short of the Creator's original plan.

In the 23rd chapter of Leviticus, God explains His schedule for the year. Actually, as we will cover in a later chapter, this schedule is really His plan for all time and the agenda for the Messiah. But the relevance to our topic here is that at the beginning of the chapter, God tells Moses that He is going to give him the list of Feasts:

> *And the* LORD *spoke to Moses, saying, "Speak to the children of Israel, and say to them: 'The feasts of the* LORD, *which you shall proclaim to be holy convocations, these are My feasts.'* "[21]

Notice the LORD does not say, *"these are the feasts of Israel,"* but *"these are MY feasts."* We will cover this in more detail later, but the Hebrew word translated as 'feasts' is *moedim*, (sing. *mo'ed*) which more correctly means 'appointed times.' In our modern vernacular, we would say this is God's appointment calendar. They are specific times on His schedule that He has scheduled appointments to interact with creation, especially His people. The first scheduled appointment on His list is the Sabbath:

> *"Six days shall work be done, but the seventh day is a Sabbath of solemn rest, a holy convocation. You shall do no work on it; it is the Sabbath of the* LORD *in all your dwellings."*[22]

If you ask a Jewish person, who is even moderately familiar with his religious heritage, which is the holiest day of the year, he will tell you that it is the Sabbath. Even *Yom Kippur* (Day of Atonement), with all its reverence and solemnity is considered less holy than the Sabbath. Why? Because the LORD put the

---

[21] Lev. 23:1-2
[22] Lev. 23:3

Sabbath at the top of His list of appointed times.

God does not forget an appointment. Does that mean He isn't around on Sunday? No, but it isn't the same. The Sabbath carries a special blessing with it, one that cannot be experienced on the other days of the week.

The third important word in this fourth commandment is 'keep.' Having already blessed and sanctified the seventh day (i.e., made it holy) at the time of creation, it is given to man to *keep* it holy. It is not our responsibility to do something to make it holy, nor can our actions make any other day holy. It is incumbent upon us to monitor our behaviour and speech in order to safeguard the uniqueness of the Sabbath day.

The fourth word I wish to highlight from Exodus 20:8 is 'holy.' In its simplest terms, the Hebrew word *kadosh*, here translated as 'holy,' means 'set apart' in the sense of being set apart for God's. An integral part of Sabbath is distinguishing it as different from the other six days of the week, and doing so primarily by setting it aside to meet with God among His people. It is a time for listening to His voice through the apostles and prophets of old in the pages of Scripture. It is to be a day of 'holy convocation'—gathering together unto Him.

The Jewish way of setting the Sabbath apart begins on Friday evening at sundown. There is a special meal, always different, but always containing bread and wine. Bread and wine is the covenant meal, instituted by Melchizedek back in Genesis 14:18-20. There is a time of blessings; the father blesses the sons, the mother blesses the daughters and then the parents bless each other. The remainder of the Sabbath until sundown Saturday is spent in fellowship and learning from the Word of God. Finally, after three stars have appeared on Saturday evening, the Sabbath is closed with the extinguishing of a special braided candle in an overflowing cup of wine and prayers for the coming week. In every way it is different from the rest of the week.

The modern Christian argument that Sunday is now the Sabbath is nullified by their actions on that day. A generation or two ago, Sundays were at least set as a day of rest; today it is just the second day of the weekend punctuated with a one-, or at the most, a two-hour service at church. The aspects of doing no work or not making anyone else have to work (such as store clerks or waitresses) that are integral to Sabbath are disregarded.

This same evidence also negates the claim that now every day is a Sabbath day. The Hebrew word *Shabbat* or Sabbath as we know it, means 'to rest' or 'to cease.' In Genesis 2:2-3 it says,

> *And on the seventh day God ended His work which He had done, and He rested* [Heb. Shabbat] *on the seventh day...Then God blessed the seventh day and sanctified it, because in it He rested* [Heb. Shabbat] *from all His work which God had created and made.*

The Sabbath day is set apart, made holy, sanctified—because God rested that day. He didn't rest because He was tired; He rested because He was done. There is a time coming when we will enter that Sabbath-rest the writer of Hebrews spoke about, but now is not that time. *We will enter our rest when we are done.* We still have work to do, so for now we enjoy the weekly taste of what is to come. He wrote:

> *For he who has entered his rest has himself also ceased from his works as God did from His.*[23]

For years this verse has been misapplied to believers. The context dictates that 'he who has entered his rest' is referring to *Yeshua*, not us. The verses before and after this verse say,

> *There remains therefore a rest* [Gk. *Sabbatismos*— Sabbath-keeping] *for the people of God.* (v.9)

> *Let us therefore be diligent to enter into that rest, lest anyone fall according to the same example of disobedience.* (v.11)

---

[23] Heb. 4:10

Apart from God, Yeshua is the only one who has finished His work. The author states this plainly in chapter 10:

> *But this man, after He had offered one sacrifice for sins forever, sat down at the right hand of God, from that moment waiting till His enemies are made His footstool.*[24]

Every day is not a Sabbath day; it is still our place to work six days a week.

I was dismayed as I watched what I thought were three very solid footings—those upon which the 'Christian Sabbath' is based—crumble beneath the weight of truth.

Another facet of the Sabbath

In Exodus 31 we are shown another aspect of the Sabbath:

> *And the LORD spoke to Moses, saying, "Speak to the children of Israel, saying: 'Surely My Sabbaths you shall keep, **for it is a sign between Me and you throughout your generations**, that you may know that I am the LORD who sanctifies you. You shall keep the Sabbath, therefore, for it is holy to you. Everyone who profanes it shall surely be put to death; for whoever does any work on it, that person shall be cut off from among his people. Work shall be done for six days, but the seventh is the Sabbath of rest, holy to the LORD. Whoever does any work on the Sabbath day, he shall surely be put to death. Therefore the children of Israel shall keep the Sabbath, to observe the Sabbath throughout their generations as a perpetual covenant. **It is a sign between Me and the children of Israel forever**; for in six days the LORD made the heavens and the earth, and on the seventh day He rested and was*

---

[24] Heb.10:12-13

refreshed.'"[25] *(emphasis mine)*

Notice where I have emphasized that God says it is a sign between Him and Israel forever. The word translated as 'sign' means 'mark of distinction.' This is the same word as in Genesis 4:15 where God *'set a **mark** on Cain, lest anyone finding him should kill him.'* This tells us that the distinctive mark of identification on God's people is their adherence to and observance of the Sabbath day. Also, notice carefully the word 'forever.' Right from creation, the seventh day was His special day, and He reminded Israel of it again here. He goes even further by declaring it a capital offence to violate the Sabbath by working on it or profaning it in any way. The word 'profane' means 'to make common or ordinary.' Treating the Sabbath like any other day of the week is making it into a common thing. When we say that every day is a Sabbath, then Sabbath becomes 'everyday.'

The instruction to remember and observe the Sabbath day is repeated ten times in the *Torah.*[26] That tells me that it is something important to God. When my wife Pamela and I became aware that there might be some truth about the Sabbath, we decided to try a simple experiment: we would observe Sabbath as a day of rest for six weeks and then evaluate the effects in our lives. We were still pastoring at the time, so giving up our Saturday was not a simple matter; it effectively shortened our weekend for getting things done around the house to a half a day on Sunday. Six months later, one of us said, "Hey! I thought we were going to try this for six weeks." It had become such a blessing in our life that we were quickly 'hooked.' Pamela told me in no uncertain terms, "Don't even *think* about asking me to give up Sabbath!"

But as I thought about her statement, I realized that sometime, somehow, people *were* asked or told to give up the Sabbath. How did this happen? Why would somebody want to do that? As I said at the beginning of this chapter, there are some excellent books that document when and how it transpired. I will not try to

[25] Ex. 31:12-17
[26] Ex. 16:23-26; 20:8; 23:12; 31:12-17; 34:21; 35:2; Lev. 19:30; 23:3; 26:2; Dt. 5:12.

'reinvent the wheel' since they have done an excellent job of making the case; I will just summarize some of the details, as well as bring in some other material.

What about the early believers?

When I began my search for evidence to corroborate my belief that Sabbath was the 'Old Testament way' and that Sunday was the 'New Testament way,' I didn't get very far before I ran into a problem. The problem I encountered was the discovery that *the early believers continued to gather on the Sabbath for at least 100 years after the resurrection!* In fact, for the first few decades, believers were considered to be another sect within Judaism known as 'the Nazarenes' or 'Nazarene Judaism.'

A cursory look at the beginnings of Christianity reveals a Church that was made up exclusively of Jews. Indeed, the Church was viewed as a sect within Judaism, as the book of Acts makes clear in referring to the followers of Jesus as 'the sect of the Nazarenes' (Acts 24:5). They seemed to function easily within Judaism in that they were described as "enjoying the favour of all the people" (Acts 2:47).[27]

"The early Church up to 70 C.E. was a daughter of Judaism: only then did it leave the nest."[28]

The day of worship, as well as other practices of the Nazarenes, underwent change for two main reasons: first, the non-Jewish believers began to outnumber and overtake those of Jewish background, and second, the anti-Semitism of the Roman government. Those are the two factors that caused the major shift in Church practices.

---

[27] Marvin R. Wilson, *Our Father Abraham*; Jewish Roots of the Christian Faith (Grand Rapids: William B. Eerdmans Publishing Co., 1989), p. 41

[28] ibid. p.77, quoted from W. D. Davies, *Paul and Rabbinic Judaism*, 4th ed. (Philadelphia: Fortress Press, 1980), p. *xxxviii*.

At the time of Messiah, the Roman government showed tolerance to the Jews in allowing them to continue—for the most part—their religion. Judaism was an 'approved religion' along with Roman religion of worshipping Zeus and the pantheon of gods. So when Christianity came along, they were 'grandfathered' under the umbrella of Judaism. However, within thirty years, Rome had appointed governors over the Jews who were less than tolerant of their ways. Eventually, Rome itself began to restrict and punish the Jews 'and those who live like Jews.' The phrase 'and those who live like Jews' was added so as to include non-Jewish Messianic believers. It was this persecution of the Jews that led to the rebellion that resulted in the destruction of the temple in 70 C.E. It also led to the first split between Jewish and non-Jewish believers, because the non-Jews availed themselves of the opportunity to distance themselves from their Jewish brethren. Having once claimed asylum within Judaism from Rome's interference, now they claimed separation from Judaism to escape Rome's fury.

Of course, the Jewish believers couldn't claim to be non-Jewish (nor would they want to), so they were forced to suffer at the hands of their oppressors along with non-believing Jews. It was during this time the familiar 'throwing the Christians to the lions' is known to have taken place.

This persecution of the Jews waxed and waned during the next few decades, but reached a fever pitch under the Roman emperor Hadrian around the year 130 C.E. It was at this time a Jewish man named Simon bar Kosiba rose up to lead a rebellion against Rome and free the Jews for good. The leading rabbi in Israel at that time, Rabbi Akiva, declared bar Kosiba to be the Messiah[29] and gave him the name bar Kochba (Son of a Star) to

---

[29] In order to support his Messianic proclamation of bar Kosiba, Rabbi Akiva had to 'adjust' the Jewish calendar by many years in order to have the 'Messiah' born at the right time according to Jewish expectation. Both bar Kosiba and Rabbi Akiva were killed during the rebellion, but the calendar was never corrected. The Jewish leaders didn't set the calendar back because it would have given support to the claim of Yeshua ben Joseph of Nazareth as being the Messiah, because He *was* born at the right time. See *Exploring the World of the Jew* by John Philips (Chicago, Moody Press 1927, rev. 1981), p. 78

fulfil Balaam's prophecy in Numbers 24:17,

> *"I see Him, but not now;*
> *I behold Him, but not near;*
> *A star shall come out of Jacob,*
> *A Sceptre shall rise out of Israel,*
> *And batter the brow of Moab,*
> *And destroy all the sons of tumult."*

The Jewish believers who were sympathetic to the cause up until that point, could no longer be in support of it because they knew that Messiah had come one hundred years earlier. This, then, was the final rift between Judaism and Nazarene Judaism/Christianity. Since that time there has been resentment, animosity, and many times, brutal violence between them.

Although they were now severed from Judaism, those Jewish believers and their successors continued to follow the teachings of the apostles: to observe the Sabbath day and the Feasts of the LORD, and to obey the Law of Moses. Meanwhile, non-Jewish 'Christianity,' as it was now called, was beginning to drift from the prescribed course. Having abandoned the practice of the Sabbath day and other 'Jewish' practices, for security reasons, it was forced to lay new foundations and establish new traditions.

Constantine to the 'rescue!'

The last remaining vestiges of the Hebraic roots of the Church were cut off under the influence of the Roman Emperor Constantine in 325 C.E. Having allegedly seen a vision of the sign of the cross in the sky, and subsequently 'converted to Christianity,' he not only legalized the religion, he made it the official religion of the Empire. Many historians now look at this change of affairs as a purely political move to unite the growing factions within his empire. It is well documented that Constantine remained a sun-worshipper until the day he died.

While claiming to be a 'Christian,' Constantine maintained the title "Pontifus Maximus" the high priest of paganism. His coins were inscribed: "*SOL INVICTO COMITI*" (committed to the invincible sun).[30]

Constantine, **while claiming to be a Christian**, recognized the sun as his guide and protector, the patron of his power (fautori imperii sui), ordered his wife and son murdered, and had a column and statue erected depicting himself as Apollo the sun-god. The remains of the column can still be seen in Istanbul, Turkey: remains only, for it was struck by lightning and is now referred to as 'the burnt column.'[31]

However, he soon discovered that there was not even a clear unity within Christianity. (Amazing!) To bring about a single doctrine and purpose within the Church, he gathered at his own expense all of the prominent bishops and elders from as far away as Spain and Africa to hammer out a consensus of faith. A footnote to this otherwise commendable gesture is that the delegates were all non-Jewish.

The effects of the gathering, known in history as the First Ecumenical Council, or The Council of Nicea, would alter Christianity forever. One of the decisions ratified by that council was the absolute rejection of the seventh-day Sabbath for worship and the establishment of the first day of the week as its replacement. Although the practice had begun among non-Jewish believers in the late first century, this edict made it compulsory upon all who wished to be counted among the Church.

Biblical Sabbath observance within the church continued until the time of Constantine when Sunday, the Lord's Day (a name given to the first day of the week in honour of the Roman Emperor—literally 'Imperial Day') was

---

[30] Richard M. Reves, *Too Long in the Sun* (Charlotte: Partakers Publications, 2001), p. 66
[31] ibid. p. 228

substituted for the Sabbath. The church council of Nicea in 325 "widened the breach between Christianity and Judaism by forbidding the celebration of the Christian Sabbath on Saturday and tried to prevent the coincidence of Easter and Passover."[32]

Even W.E. Vine, in his classic work, *Vine's Expository Dictionary of New Testament Words*, acknowledged:

For the first three centuries of the Christian era the first day of the week was never confounded with the Sabbath; the confusion of the Jewish and Christian institutions was due to declension from apostolic teaching.[33]

Among other dogmas established during this council was the pre-eminence of the bishop of Rome over the whole Church. Thus was born the Roman Catholic (universal) Church. Ironically, Rome, which had persecuted the Jews politically and militarily, would again take up the position 'under sheep's clothing.'

Then came the 'Reformation'…

Fast-forwarding twelve hundred years to the time of Martin Luther, we hear of his followers being branded as 'protestants,' i.e., protestors. Luther didn't pick this label; the Catholic Church pinned it on them. It is meant in the sense of 'protesting Catholics,' but as I pointed out in a previous chapter, their protest wasn't complete.

In the mid-sixteenth century, the Roman Catholic Church convened a council in an effort to strengthen their position doctrinally and administratively against Protestantism. This council, the Council of Trent, was for the purpose of formulating doctrines in the spirit of counter-reformation. At this council, the

---

[32] *The New Standard Jewish Encyclopedia*, p. 214

[33] W.E. Vine, *Vine's Expository Dictionary of New Testament Words, p. 994*

papal representative, the Archbishop of Reggio, presented his argument denouncing the Reformers' claim of *sola Scriptura*—that they stand on Scripture alone.

> "The Protestants claim to stand on the written Word only; they profess to hold to the Scriptures alone as the standard of faith; they justify their revolt by the plea that the Church has apostasized from the written Word and follows tradition. The Protestants' claim that they stand upon the written Word alone is not true; their profession of holding the Scriptures alone as the standard of faith is false. Here is proof:

> "The Word explicitly enjoins the observance of the seventh day as the Sabbath; they do not observe the seventh day but reject it. If they truly hold the Scriptures alone as the standard, they would be observing the seventh day as it is enjoined in the Scriptures throughout. Yet they not only reject the observance of the Sabbath as enjoined in the written Word, but they have adopted, and do practice, the observance of Sunday, for which they have only the tradition of the [Roman Catholic] Church.

> "Consequently, the claim of Scripture alone as the standard fails, and the doctrine of 'Scripture and tradition as essential' is fully established, the Protestants themselves being judges."

Even today, this evidence is still bearing witness of Protestant Christianity's association with the Roman Catholic Church and disassociation with the teaching of Scripture.

Consider this example from the Catholic catechism:

> Sunday is our mark of authority. This transference of the Sabbath to Sunday as the day of worship is proof of the fact that we [the Roman Catholic Church] have

supremacy over the canon of Scripture. It is proof also that the Protestant religions accept our authority as they all recognize the authority of the Roman Catholic Church and observe the Sunday day of worship.

Or this statement from the book *The Faith of Our Fathers* by Cardinal James Gibbons:

You may read the Bible from Genesis to Revelation and you will not find a single line authorizing the sanctification or setting apart of Sunday. The Scriptures enforce the religious observance of Saturday, a day we never sanctified.[34]

Or this excerpt from the book *This is Our Faith*:

The Church, speaking with Divine authority, says that all her members must honour God at least weekly by the offering of sacrifice, and naturally this should be done on the day set apart by God for the purpose.

Incidentally, there is no proof in Scripture that God willed the Sabbath to be changed from Saturday to Sunday, so that those non-Catholics who do not accept the value of tradition as a source of faith should logically still observe Saturday as the Sabbath.[35]

One last possibility

For me, the sheer weight of evidence had obliterated all my arguments and suppositions about Sunday having replaced the Sabbath. I was left with one last possibility, one glimmer of hope that could salvage the issue: how do we know that the day we call

---

[34] Gibbons, Cardinal James; *The Faith of Our Fathers Being a Plain Exposition and Vindication of the Church Founded by Our Lord Jesus Christ* (Baltimore, John Murray, 1905)

[35] Pennock, Michael; *This is Our Faith: Correlated & Referenced to the Catechism of the Catholic Church* (Ave Maria Press 1998), p. 176

the Sabbath (Saturday) today is the correct day? Maybe over the centuries people lost track and the real Sabbath is now Tuesday, or maybe Sunday.

I chased this notion, but again, my hope was short-lived. I was given an article written by a scientist who had 'rewound' the astronomical clock—the clock of the stars and planets—and verified that the days we recognize now correspond exactly with the same days in recorded ancient history. I couldn't really understand everything in the article, but his conclusion was clearly stated.

I know also that when Yeshua was on earth, He would have observed the correct Sabbath. He doesn't have any qualms about the particular day being observed during the first century C.E. Since His time, there has been an abundance of recorded history that verifies the chronology up to the present. Even when the secular calendar was changed under Pope Gregory XIII in 1582 and 10 days were eliminated to bring the seasons back into alignment, only the date was changed, not the day of the week; i.e., Oct. 4th, 1582 was followed by Oct. 15th. Sabbath has not been mislabelled as another day of the week.

My study of the Sabbath brought me to a conclusion I never expected to reach. I had tested every premise that upholds the practice of Sunday and found them to be mere pretences. I could find no supporting evidence for a Scripturally-based discontinuation of the observance of the seventh-day Sabbath. I reasoned that surely God in His foreknowledge would have foreseen the need to honour the first day of the week and given it the pre-eminence from the beginning. He had foreseen the location of Messiah's crucifixion and instructed Abraham to offer Isaac on the very site; He had prefigured the time of year for the crucifixion in the slaying of the Passover lamb whose blood brought deliverance from the death angel. Yet not a hint of the cessation of the Sabbath, either for another day or altogether.

The Resurrection was not a rejection of the Sabbath

I discovered that the resurrection of Yeshua after the completion of the Sabbath was not a statement by God that the Sabbath was now superseded; it was set to occur then because the day after the Sabbath after Passover is the day of Firstfruits,[36] when the first sheaf of ripe grain is waved before the LORD. The apostle Paul alludes to this in 1 Cor. 15:20-23:

> *"But now Messiah is risen from the dead, and has become* ***the firstfruits*** *of those who have fallen asleep. For since by man came death, by man also came the resurrection of the dead. For as in Adam all die, even so in Messiah all shall be made alive. But each one in his own order:* ***Messiah the first fruits,*** *afterward those who are Messiah's at His coming."* (emphasis mine)

Choose you THIS day

I was left with a choice: either believing I had discovered the truth and then acting upon it, or disregarding my discovery for the comfort and security offered by 1700 years of tradition. The decision was relatively easy based on the undisputable evidence; the price, however, was relatively high. Even greater are the rewards that God has given to us for obeying His word and honouring His Sabbath day.

---

[36] See chapter 5.

Chapter 4
From Yeshua to Jesus

The very name 'Christianity' implies a domain of 'Christians,' a name that was pinned on the followers of 'Christ' first in Antioch, Syria during the first century.[1]   The title 'Christian,' although it probably originally had a derogatory tone of sarcasm attached to it, depicted one who was trying to be a 'little Christ.' In present-day jargon they would be called 'Christ wannabes.' Those early believers accepted and wore the moniker with pride, happy to be associated with their King and Master. Indeed it was their aim to be like Him—to live as He lived—even as we are exhorted by John:

> *"He who says he abides in Him ought himself to walk just as He walked."[2]*

But that apparently simple instruction begs the question: "How did He walk, i.e., live?" This is without doubt the most crucial question for us to answer, because until that issue is resolved we cannot hope to be like Messiah. According to the late Dr. Walter Martin of 'The Bible Answer Man' fame, the fundamental difference between a cult and mainstream Christianity is the 'Jesus' they believe in and emulate. In his classic reference work *The Kingdom of the Cults*, he devoted an entire chapter to 'the Jesus of the cults' to expose the impostors. He wrote:

> Since the earliest days of Christianity, both apostle and disciple alike have been confronted with the perversion of the revelation God has given us in the person of Jesus Christ. This perversion has extended historically, not just to the teaching of our Lord, but more important, to the Person of Christ; *for it is axiomatic that if the doctrine of*

---

[1] Acts 11:26
[2] 1 John 2:6

Christ Himself, i.e., His Person, nature and work are perverted, so the identity of the life-giver is altered, then the life which He came to give is correspondingly negated. And it is at precisely this juncture that in this day and age, we come face to face with the phenomenon that the apostle Paul described in 2 Corinthians chapter 11 as "the other Jesus." [3] (emphasis mine)

The person and work of Christ is indeed the very foundation of Christian faith. *And if it is redefined and interpreted out of context and therefore contrary to its Biblical content, the whole message of the Gospel is radically altered and its value correspondingly diminished.* The early apostles clearly saw this, as did John and Jude, hence their repeated emphasis upon maintaining the identity and ministry of the historical Jesus over against the counterfeits of that Person already beginning to arise in their own era.[4] (emphasis mine)

These statements express succinctly the importance of a correct understanding of not only who He was, but equally as important, what He came to do and teach His followers. Without that proper foundation, we are adrift on a sea of well-defined, but erroneous, premises.

I had already begun to clue in on the anti-Semitic propensity of the post-apostolic Church, and now I began to ponder the veracity of the Jesus in whom I believed and trusted. Could this ancient prejudice against all things Jewish have made way for a misrepresentation of Him in the systematic theology of the Church that has been handed down for generations? If it had, what effect has it had on the true gospel of the kingdom? More importantly, if the image of Messiah has been altered, what is His true character, and what is His message? I began a quest to meet

---

[3] Dr. Walter Martin, *The Kingdom of the Cults* (Minneapolis, Bethany House Publishers, revised and expanded edition – 1985), p. 377

[4] ibid. p. 378

the Saviour and make my own determination on whether His identity had been changed.

Putting 'Jesus' in context

I began by putting Him back into His proper context of history and culture. The name He bore while on earth was not 'Jesus.' That is the Anglicized version of the Grecian name *Iesous* which, when pronounced, sounds like 'yay-zeus.'[5] The name He was given by His heavenly Father was 'Yeshua,' which means 'God is salvation.' That is why the angel's message to Joseph was:

> *"And you shall call His name Yeshua, for He shall save His people from their sins."*[6]

His name stated His mission; He became the embodiment of the salvation of God.

In one discussion with some religious Jews, Yeshua told them,

> *"If you believed Moses, you would believe Me, for he wrote about Me."*[7]

One doesn't have to look very hard to find reference in the Pentateuch to 'the salvation of the LORD.' For example, after the Israelites had arrived at the Red Sea and were being pursued by the Egyptian army, to dispel the growing panic among the people Moses said, *"Stand still and see the salvation* (Yeshua) *of the LORD."*[8] All throughout the Prophets and the Psalms, 'the salvation of the LORD' is mentioned as a prophetic foreshadow of Yeshua and His ministry.

The word 'Christ' is also an Anglicization of the Greek word

---

[5] It is worth noting that the name 'Jesus' does not mean anything in any known language.
[6] Mat. 1:21
[7] John 5:46
[8] Ex. 14:13

Christos, which is supposedly a translation of the Hebrew word *Mashiach*—Messiah, the anointed One. [9] So the person whom I had always known as Jesus Christ was actually *Yeshua HaMashiach.*

This may sound like an inconsequential detail, but for me it was a doorway to discovery about who He was/is and what He came to do. Growing up in a Christian home, I was well acquainted with Jesus; we had pictures of Him on the walls, we had Bible story books with His picture in them, and I went to Sunday school every week where I saw Him in the flannel-graph lessons. Yes sir, I could recognize Jesus anywhere. He was the one with the perfect Caucasian complexion, the flowing blond hair and blue eyes.[10] As I grew up, my understanding of Him advanced beyond physical appearance to a fuller knowledge of His character, His likes and dislikes and His religious orientation. The Jesus I knew was a blond-haired, blue-eyed, pork-eating, Sabbath-breaking, White Anglo-Saxon Protestant. He fit in very well in the large middle-class Caucasian-dominated Protestant church we attended. Sure, I knew He lived among the Jews; you couldn't read the gospels without knowing that they argued with Him constantly and frustrated Him perpetually. And, of course, they were the ones who killed Him in the end.

But when it really dawned on me that He *was* a Jew,

---

[9] I say supposedly because that is the way it is used in the Greek texts. However, the word *Christos* is borrowed from Greek mythology, which got it from the mythology of ancient India where it appeared as *Chrishna* or *Krishna*. In Alexander Hislop's *The Two Babylons*, Krishna is depicted as the one who crushes the serpent's head with his foot. (Sound familiar?)

[10] It is interesting to discover a less well-known description of 'Jesus.' In their commentary on Isaiah 53, Keil and Delitzch wrote: "The Church before Constantine pictured to itself the Lord, as He walked on earth, as repulsive in appearance; whereas the Church after Constantine pictured Him as having quite an ideal beauty." (Vol. II, pg. 307, note 1) *Smith's Dictionary of Christian Antiquities* provides a number of historical references to show that the early fathers of the Church (before the time of Constantine) were well aware (and believed) that Jesus was repulsive in appearance. (Vol. I, p. 875) "Not only did they begin to make Him handsome, they put long hair on Him that closely resembled pagan gods and early philosophers…Having long hair and a beard were marks of Gentile philosophers and also pagan gods, but this is how people in post-Constantine times began to imagine Jesus groomed Himself. (Ernest L. Martin, *Secrets of Golgotha*; ASK Publications, 1988; p. 217-218)

completely Jewish, I realized that I wasn't very familiar with Him at all. He had spent His life attempting to *convince* His people, not *condemn* them. The angel's prophetic announcement to Joseph about the child Mary would bear was: *"...for He shall save His people from their sins."* (emphasis mine) They were His people because He was one of them. He was not sent to bring an end to all things Jewish; He was sent to bring an end to their misunderstanding of God and His ways.

What 'led' you to Messiah?

In order to meet Yeshua HaMashiach, there is a process that has been set in place: a person must be introduced to Him. I don't mean that someone must attend an evangelistic 'crusade' or even have another person 'lead them to Jesus.' Rabbi Sha'ul, more commonly known as the Apostle Paul, hints at the protocol in Galatians 3:23-24:

> But before faith came, we were kept under guard by the law (Torah), *kept for the faith that would afterward be revealed. Therefore **the law was our tutor to bring us to Messiah,** that we might be justified by faith.* (emphasis mine)

The Greek word translated as 'tutor' in these verses is *paidogogous* and it has been mistranslated in most English Bibles as 'schoolmaster' or, as I have quoted from the NKJV, 'tutor.' A better translation would be 'guide' or 'guardian.' *Thayer's Greek-English Lexicon of the New Testament* defines *paidogogous* in this way:

> Among the Greeks and Romans the name was applied to trustworthy slaves who were charged with the duty of supervising the life and morals of boys belonging to the better class. The boys were not allowed so much as to step out of the house without them before arriving at the

age of manhood.[11]

Along with mistranslation comes the misrepresentation of the law as being so severe that we are relieved to be out from under its constraints thanks to Messiah. But equally as misunderstood in the verse is that the main function of the law was to bring us to Messiah; the law was given as the agent through which we would come to know Him. Yeshua said, *"Moses wrote about Me,"* therefore the only way we can be sure if the Messiah we believe in is the right one is to measure Him by the description found in the *Torah*.

Many people who believe in Jesus today have arrived at their conclusion some other way; some were born into a believing family and just followed in their parents' footsteps; some turned their life over to Him as a result of a personal catastrophe, e.g., "God, I promise I'll serve you for the rest of my life if you get me out of this mess;" others were persuaded at an emotionally vulnerable time in their life. But the more important question is not whether a person believes in the Saviour, but rather is the Saviour in whom he believes the One about whom Moses—as well as the prophets— wrote?

The Messiah of the Scriptures

From the time Adam and Eve were in the Garden of Eden, there was a promise of a Saviour—a Messiah. Through the process of progressive revelation, details were added to the picture until there was a 'composite sketch' of the One to come. Some details were given in a prefigure, or type, such as when Abraham took Isaac up Mt. Moriah, or the events of Joseph's life. Other details came in the form of spoken prophecy. Whichever method God used, the fact remained that the specifics had to be fulfilled.

I readily acknowledge there is some common ground between Jesus whom I had come to know at a young age and Yeshua whom I know now. The domain of which I was completely

---

[11] *Thayer's Greek-English Lexicon of the New Testament*, p. 472

unaware is the vital discrepancy between the two. As could be expected, that discrepancy is rooted in His Jewishness. As I pointed out above, the Jews of two thousand years ago—who, incidentally, were expecting the Messiah to arrive at that time— would have been examining any and all who claimed to be the Messiah (and there were others) against the Law and the Prophets. But tantamount to fulfilling the details completely, they were looking to see if the man would follow the Law perfectly. The Jewish expectation was—and still is—that Messiah would come and correct their misunderstandings of *Torah*. But of paramount importance is that anyone claiming to be Messiah would not contradict or abolish even 'the least stroke of a pen' of the *Torah*.

The question was put to John the Baptizer by the priests and Levites sent to examine him, *"Are you the Prophet?"* [12] He had just denied being the Messiah or Elijah, so they asked him if he might be another figure they were expecting. This expectation was based on a prophecy of Moses' recorded in Deuteronomy 18:15-19:

> *"The* LORD *your God will raise up for you a Prophet like me from your midst, from your brethren. Him you shall hear, according to all that you desired of the* LORD *your God in Horeb in the day of the assembly, saying, 'Let me not hear again the voice of the* LORD *my God, not let me see this great fire anymore, lest I die.'*
> *"And the* LORD *said to me: 'What they have spoken is good. I will raise up for them a Prophet like you from among their brethren, and will put My words in His mouth, and He shall speak to them all that I command Him. And it shall be that whoever will not hear My words, which He speaks in My name, I will require it of him.'"*

We know this to be a reference to Yeshua as 'the Prophet like Moses.' The ancient Jewish sages also realized it was an allusion

---

[12] John 1:19-21

to the Messiah, even to the point that they not only expected Messiah to communicate with the LORD face to face as Moses did,[13] but that his life would also parallel the life of Moses.

A very conspicuous clue is given by Moses, which positively identifies Yeshua as the Prophet who was raised up in Moses' stead, whose life paralleled his—even to the point of being the anointed deliverer/saviour of the nation. When we consider that Moses communicated with God face to face, it does not seem at all unusual that God would disclose to him the name of the One to come. Without blurting out the divine secret to which he had been made privy, Moses subtly revealed it to those who are observant. Just prior to sending the twelve spies into Canaan, Moses did something that was seemingly insignificant but actually profoundly prophetic. He chose a man named Hoshea to represent the tribe of Ephraim, but then changed Hoshea's name to Joshua (Yeshua).[14] Joshua had been a personal servant to Moses before this; he had led the Israelite army against the Amalekites, and he had escorted Moses up Mt. Sinai when God gave him the Ten Commandments. Moses knew that this man would be his successor in leading the nation, and he also knew the name of his spiritual successor—the true deliverer and prophet like himself— so he prophetically gave him the name Joshua, 'Yeshua.' In fact, the translators who worked on the *Septuagint* wrote his name in Greek as *Iesous,* exactly the same name as the name in the Greek New Testament that became 'Jesus.'

If you look at Hebrews 4:8, this synonymy of these two characters has created some uncertainty about which one of them is being spoken of:

> *"For if Joshua had given them rest, then He would not have afterward spoken of another day."*

The marginal note in my Bible says about the name 'Joshua:'

---

[13] In Numbers 12:6-8 the LORD declared that only to Moses would He speak face to face; with any other prophet He would communicate through visions, dreams or dark sayings, i.e., riddles.

[14] Num. 13:16

"Grk. *Jesus*, same as Heb. *Joshua*." Moses was right.

How to recognize a false prophet

Most Christians have heard something to the effect of God commanding Israel to stone false prophets. Usually, however, their understanding of how a false prophet was exposed is limited to whether or not what was prophesied came to pass. That is *one* of the criteria used in judgment. But what if the matter predicted was for the distant future, or even the 'last days?' How could the prophet be evaluated on that evidence?

The book of Deuteronomy is the record of Moses' last instructions to Israel before he was taken from them. In this final address, there is a clear directive given for just such a case:

> *"If there arises among you a prophet or dreamer of dreams, and he gives you a sign or a wonder, and the sign or wonder comes to pass, of which he spoke to you, saying, 'Let us go after other gods'—which you have not known— and let us serve them,' you shall not listen to the words of that prophet or that dreamer of dreams,* **for the Lord your God is testing you, to know whether you love the Lord your God with all your heart and with all your soul.** *You shall walk after the Lord your God and fear Him, and keep His commandments and obey His voice: you shall serve Him and hold fast to Him. But that prophet or that dreamer of dreams shall be put to death, because he has spoken in order to turn you away from the Lord your God who brought you out of the land of Egypt and redeemed you from the house of bondage,* **to entice you from the way in which the Lord your God commanded you to walk.** *So you shall put away the evil from your midst."* [15](emphasis mine)

This is a distinct warning to the people not to be swayed by

---

[15] Dt. 13:1-5

signs and wonders—however amazing they may be—but to judge the prophets by their teaching, specifically whether or not that prophet was trying to entice them away from '*the way in which the* LORD *your God commanded you to walk,*' i.e., to keep His commandments. Even more sobering is the statement that the LORD would allow prophets like that to arise to test whether the people really loved the LORD with all their heart or not.

This benchmark would have been used, or at least it *should* have been used, on every prophet from that time forward, and it certainly would have been used on Yeshua. When one examines the biblical Jewish Yeshua according to this standard, you discover that He was a true prophet who observed and taught the commandments of God. Even Rabbi Moses ben Maimon (1135-1204; a.k.a. 'Maimonides' or 'the Rambam') who is regarded as one of, if not *the* greatest rabbi of the last two millennia, believed that Yeshua was one who kept the Law—including the Sabbath— although he did not accept Yeshua's Messianic claims.

It appears that some of Yeshua's detractors were slandering Him and disseminating information that He was a false prophet who was teaching contrary to the *Torah*. Why else would He be so adamant to set the record straight in Matthew 5:17-19?

> "*Do not think that I came to destroy the Law or the Prophets. I did not come to destroy but to fulfil. For assuredly I say to you, till heaven and earth pass away, one jot or one tittle will by no means pass from the Law till all is fulfilled. Whoever therefore breaks one of the least of these commandments, and teaches men so, shall be called least in the kingdom of heaven; but whoever does and teaches them, he shall be called great in the kingdom of heaven.*"

We will look at these verses in more detail in chapter 8, but for now we will point out that all through the gospels there is evidence of Yeshua obeying and teaching the commandments of God—the ones in the *Torah*. In the rest of His sermon following the above quote,[16] He proceeded to strengthen the position of *Torah*, not undermine it! He didn't say, "You have heard it said, 'you shall not commit adultery,' but I say to you that it's OK every once in awhile now." He didn't diminish any of the requirements of the Law; He expanded them! In His conclusion of this 'clarification of *Torah*,' He gave a preview of the day when He sits in judgment over the kingdom. He said,

> *"Many will say to me in that day, 'Lord, Lord, have we not prophesied in your name, cast out demons in your name, and done many wonders in your name?' And then I will declare to them, 'I never knew you. Depart from Me, you who practice lawlessness.'"*[17]

Some versions translate that last word as 'iniquity,' but 'lawlessness' or 'without the law' is the proper translation of the Greek word *anomia*.

Another example is found in His encounter with the rich young ruler. When the young man asks Yeshua, *"What must I do to inherit eternal life?"* Yeshua responded by saying, *"Keep the commandments."*[18]

The True High Priest

The theme of the book of Hebrews is centered around the Day of Atonement and its ceremonies. The most important events of that day are the occasions when the High Priest enters the Holy of Holies to bring the blood of the atonement or covering. The writer of Hebrews reveals that the High Priest for all those centuries was only a prefigure of the true High Priest, Yeshua, who would enter the Holy of Holies with His own sacrificial blood. But incumbent upon every High Priest from Aaron to Yeshua was the fact that he had more commandments to observe

---

[16] commonly called 'the Sermon on the Mount,' found in Matt. 5, 6, & 7.
[17] Matt. 7:22-23
[18] Matt. 19:16-22

than any other person. Not every commandment applied to everyone, but the High Priest bore the greatest responsibility. In order for Yeshua to be qualified as High Priest, He had to keep the commandments. The emergence of the High Priest from the Holy of Holies gave testimony to the approval of the sacrifice and the priest by God. It was the yearly foreshadowing of Yeshua's resurrection; His emergence from the grave was the Father's stamp of approval on His life and sacrifice.

Putting 'Jesus' to the test

When I subjected the Jesus I had met in Christianity to Moses' 'prophet test,' on the other hand, he didn't fare so well. It seemed he had no conviction regarding obedience to any set of regulations and no reverence for one day above any other. Most importantly, the empirical evidence indicated that he taught his followers to disregard and abandon *Torah* like a sinking ship. Of course, we have no textual proof of that, but the outworking of his teaching resulted in the Church doing precisely that.

Humanly speaking, we tend to see things in shades of 'grey.' God, however, sees things as 'black or white.' From His perspective, if a person is not following His ways, they are following after another god; there is no middle ground. Therefore, any prophet—even if his name is Jesus—teaches anything but what God spoke to Moses, he should be regarded as an impostor. If this is what Jesus taught, then the Jews were absolutely justified in condemning him to death. Since the resurrection proved the death of Messiah to be unmerited, we must conclude that He did not teach divergence from the Law.

One set of commandments

Another line of argument in favour of a *Torah*-teaching Yeshua can be based on His unity with His Father. He said, *"I and My Father are one."*[19] *"I only speak what I hear My Father*

---

[19] Jn. 10:30

saying."[20] In one conversation with some religious leaders, He said, "Before Abraham was, I AM."[21] Was He merely saying that He was over two thousand years old but He just looked good for His age? No, He was saying that the One who was in Him was the I AM, the One who was in the beginning and who spoke to Moses on the mountain. The religious leaders had no doubt this was what He meant because they immediately picked up stones to execute Him for blasphemy.

We who believe the gospel writers have no trouble understanding why He said that. After all, John wrote:

"In the beginning was the Word, and the Word was with God, and the Word was God."[22]

Somehow lost in the shuffle is the inconsistency of believing that Jesus is one with the Father while at the same time believing that He came and said something diametrically opposite to what His Father had said. Even more obvious incongruities surface when it is realized that the *I AM* who spoke with Moses on the mountain from the burning bush and who later spoke the Ten Commandments to Moses was the same one speaking that day to those religious leaders.

So strong was Yeshua's passion to see His followers continue in those commandments and continue to teach others to do the same, that He said it one last time before His ascension, just to make sure they'd gotten the message. It reminds me of going over instructions to the babysitter just before we would leave for the evening. If it's the last thing they hear, we think there will be less chance of them forgetting. We know these last minute instructions to the disciples as 'the Great Commission.' He said,

"All authority has been given to Me in heaven and on earth. Go therefore and make disciples of all the nations,

---

[20] Jn. 12:50
[21] Jn. 8:58
[22] John 1:1

*baptizing them in the name of the Father and of the Son
and of the Holy Spirit, **teaching them to obey all things
that I have commanded you;** and lo, I am with you
always, even to the end of the age."*[23] (emphasis mine)

What are *"all things that I have commanded you?"* The word
'commanded' is a hint; He was indicating the commandments that
He had given through Moses. How can I be so sure? First,
Yeshua only gave one new commandment—*"that you love one
another as I have loved you, that you also love one another."*[24]
Everything else He told them to do was rooted in *Torah*. Second,
as discussed earlier, Yeshua and His Father are one; therefore
Yeshua's commandments are God's commandments. If not, then
God is double-minded.

To say that Yeshua said something different than the Father,
one must hold the position that God changed His mind, His plan,
or that He just changed—period. Of course, when it's stated so
bluntly, any Christian would recoil with denial. After all, God
Himself said,

"For I am the LORD, I do not change."[25]

And the writer of Hebrews wrote:

*"Yeshua HaMashiach, the same yesterday, today and
forever."*[26]

And Ya'akov (James) wrote:

*"...the Father of lights, with whom there is no variation or
shadow of turning."*[27]

---

[23] Matt. 28:18-20
[24] John 13:34
[25] Mal. 3:6
[26] Heb. 13:8
[27] Jas. 1:17

The Great 'Omission' from the Great Commission

If Christians know God doesn't change, how can they reconcile that knowledge with the totally new agenda that Jesus supposedly brought? The Great Commission, then, is Yeshua's 'passing of the baton' to His emissaries. He commissioned them to do exactly as He had done: make disciples and teach them to obey the commandments. It was actually a common practice of that time; rabbis (teachers) trained a select group of followers who could then, in turn, train others. Peter's brother Andrew had previously been a disciple of John the Baptizer.[28] The apostle Sha'ul (Paul) had been a disciple of Gamaliel;[29] Sha'ul then discipled Timothy and Titus, and he instructed Timothy:

> *"And the things that you have heard from me among many witnesses, commit these to faithful men who will be able to teach others also."*[30]

The object of the exercise is to pass on what you have learned.

To be a disciple of Yeshua, then, means that you follow in His footsteps. Even those who advocate that Jesus brought the Law to an end by 'fulfilling it,' i.e., doing it all, are acknowledging that He *did* follow the Law. As mentioned previously, John put it in very simple terms for us:

> *"He who says he abides in Him ought to walk just as He walked."*

Sha'ul said it another way:

> *"Imitate me as I also imitate Messiah."*[31]

The goal of being a disciple is to be like Him; to do what He

---

[28] John 1:40
[29] Acts 22:3
[30] 2 Tim. 2:2
[31] 1 Cor. 11:1

did, to speak as He spoke, to teach what He taught. Realizing His context in history and His orientation of faith, I concluded that faith *in* Yeshua should not contradict the faith *of* Yeshua.

Evidence that demands a verdict

Now that I have presented a historically and biblically accurate picture of the Messiah of the Bible, you must ask yourself if this is the One you have trusted for salvation. I know it may take time to swallow and digest this information, but if the Jesus you follow is not the One who teaches the way of the LORD—the commandments of God—then you are being led astray. Those people Yeshua described as *"you who practice lawlessness"* thought they were on the right path, doing the right things. Their eternal destination was determined by their rejection of and disobedience to the Law. How could Yeshua possibly disown them for that if He had abrogated the Law and made it void? He can't. The only way He can base His verdict on that evidence is if the Law is still valid. Sadly, I see the overwhelming majority of the Church of history and today fitting the description of 'lawless.' But if we learn nothing else from the parable of the lost son, we learn of a Father who is waiting eagerly for His child to come home. As long as you are still breathing it is not too late.

One thing which comes along naturally with the awareness of the Jewishness of Messiah and knowing that we are adopted into the family—grafted in—is a love for the Jewish people. The most loving thing a person can do toward the Jews is to introduce them to their Messiah. I know there are many Christian organizations that have pursued evangelising the Jews, but if they are going to convert them to Christianity, they are going to face the wrath of God. Let me explain why.

Historically, the separation between the Jews and the Church was what saved the Jewish people from extinction, not by *annihilation*, but rather by *assimilation*. Had the Jews stayed with the Church, they would have given up the Sabbath, the Feasts and the commandments, while replacing them with Sunday, pagan celebrations and license.

These last nineteen hundred years, the Jews have rejected their Messiah—or so we have thought. In truth, the Messiah they have rejected is one of Christian invention. The Messiah Christianity presented to them—on most occasions forcefully— was a Jew-hating, commandment-breaking person like the Christians themselves. Little wonder they reject that 'Messiah,' and it's good they do because he's not the true Messiah. God will no more condemn them for rejecting that 'Jesus' than He will condemn me for rejecting the 'Jesus' of the Mormons.

Had Christianity portrayed the true Messiah Yeshua, a *Torah*-observant rabbi who came out of love for them, the pages of history would read much differently. And unless He is presented to them in that way today, they will continue to see Him as an impostor. They laugh at a Church whose 'God' was born on December 25th, the same day the ancient Greeks celebrated the birth of Ra the sun god, and the Romans celebrated the day of Saturnalia and *Sol Invictus*—the unconquered sun. (We will address these things in the next chapter)

Leading a Jew to Jesus is leading him or her in a direction contrary to the one which Moses—under God's instructions—set for them to follow. It would be causing them to stumble from the way of the LORD . When Jews are converted to Christianity, they are usually told to give up their Jewishness and adopt the customs of Christendom. ("You're a Christian now; have a ham sandwich!") This is an ironic antithesis of the error addressed by the Jerusalem council in Acts 15. The Judaizers flatly stated that Gentiles must be circumcised in order to be saved; i.e., they must first become Jewish.[32] That was at a time when Jews made up the majority of believers and were also in the positions of authority. Now, the balance is tipped sharply to the Gentile side and they say the Jews must become like them. Neither extreme is correct.

I will leave you with the challenge to put the Messiah you

---

[32] Acts 15:1 This may have been an understandable position at the beginning since Judaism was the only religion that worshipped the one true God. However, by this time this issue had been supernaturally resolved by the Holy Spirit at Cornelius' house in Acts 10:44-48.

follow to the test of Scripture and weigh the evidence: how is He telling you to live and where is He leading you?

Chapter 5
From Holy Days to Holidays

Most of us can look back over our lives and remember lots of fun and good times with our families. Whatever the occasion, a family get-together was a much-anticipated event. Children usually go through a phase when they dread these gatherings of the clan because they hate it when all the old folks say, "Look how big you've gotten! You must have grown a whole foot since the last time I saw you!" or some other variation of embarrassing remarks. Almost always, though, as a person gets older, he or she enjoys the experience more and more. The patriarchs and matriarchs of the family get a deep sense of satisfaction from seeing their children, grandchildren and maybe even great-grandchildren. Many family reunions are punctuated with the introduction of a long-lost relative or a newborn member. The old adage "blood is thicker than water" is proven time and time again as we discover that we may not like some of our relatives, but there is an inexplicable love that bonds us together.

Some of the best and most enduring memories with family are made at holiday times. Happiness and warmth are felt by all who gather together. As the father of a son who is grown and living in another city, I look forward to those visits when we can spend time with each other. They never seem to be frequent enough or last long enough; as soon as one has ended the anticipation for the next begins. I've often thought it would be great if I could plan more holidays and occasions so we could enjoy his company more often. As I reflect on those thoughts, I realize that God, our heavenly Father, loves to have His children get together with Him too. Of course He loves to spend time with each of us on our own, but His favourite times are when He can get His arms around us in a group. And since He's not only a Father but also the Ruler of the universe, He *did* plan a lot of get-togethers.

What I would like to do over the next several pages is take a look at these plans of His and then compare them to the events which Christianity endorses, to see if there is a similarity between the two. When I initially did this study I was amazed and yet troubled by what I discovered.

The True 'LORD 's Days'

The concise list and descriptions of His plans for 'family celebrations' can be found in the 23rd chapter of Leviticus. My intention here is not to go into an in-depth discussion of each individual day that is listed, but to present a more general overview of them as a whole. There are many excellent books that do a marvellous job of expounding on each one and revealing the rich symbolism hidden within the rituals and ceremonies. If further study is desired, a list of the books I have found most enlightening will be found within the bibliography of this book.

Leviticus 23 begins with God's introduction of His schedule:

> *And the LORD spoke to Moses saying, "Speak to the children of Israel, and say to them: 'The feasts of the LORD, which you shall proclaim to be holy convocations, these are My feasts.'"*[1]

The first point that He brings to their attention is that they are the 'feasts of the LORD.' The Hebrew word translated as 'feasts,' or in some versions 'festivals,' is *moedim,* which simply means 'appointed times.' In our modern vernacular we would call them appointments. God was giving them a look into His day timer and showing them His plans. These are the specific times they could expect Him to show up and the times He expected them to be there. These are *His* appointments, not Israel's. They were His long before there was an Israel, and they will still be His long after the kingdom has come on earth. As we go through this chapter, I will show you a few examples of this foundational truth.

The second important point He emphasizes is that these

---

[1] Lev. 23:1-2

appointed times are to be proclaimed as 'holy convocations' or 'holy gatherings.' The adjective 'holy' denotes that these are 'separated' from other times, distinctly different, special. 'Holy,' as mentioned in the chapter on the Sabbath, is the opposite of common or ordinary. So we see that these times are to be regarded and observed with reverence. But observing them with reverence does not necessarily mean being somber or stoic. These are times of great joy and celebration, lots of food (except on Yom Kippur—the Day of Atonement) and fun. The Hebrew word translated as 'convocations' is *miqrah* and it means 'assemblies' or 'rehearsals.' These are the specific times God wanted His people—His children—to get together. God finishes His introduction of these special times to Moses by repeating Himself so there can be no confusion about their origin or ownership: *"These are My feasts."*

From the beginning

As I mentioned above, these appointed times were on God's calendar long before there was a nation of Israel to tell about them. The first hint of this is found in the first chapter of Genesis.

> *Then God said, "Let there be lights in the firmament of the heavens to divide the day from the night; and let them be for signs and seasons, and for days and years."*[2]

While the average non-Jewish reader sees the words *signs, seasons, days,* and *years* and accepts them at face value, the person initiated into the Hebraic understanding of Scripture sees something deeper.

Signs is a figurative term for Sabbaths. This is understood from Ex. 31:13 where God tells Israel that His Sabbaths are a sign (i.e., a mark of distinction) between Him and them throughout their generations. Without the sun and the moon, the Sabbaths of the LORD could not be calculated.

---

[2] Gen. 1:14

Seasons is a term which is used to denote the appointed times and other religious occasions. The Hebrew word here is *mo'edim,* appointed times. Right from the time of creation His 'set times' are established, and the purpose for which He created the heavenly bodies was for the annunciation of those times.

Days is a Hebrew idiom for the beginnings of months. The first day of each month is to be announced and celebrated as a special day.[3] In Hebrew, the first day of each month is known as *rosh chodesh*—the 'head of the renewal.' Each month begins with the sighting of the new moon when the smallest sliver of light is seen emerging from the shadow of the earth.[4] Of course, we know that it is not a 'new moon,' but it is the same moon that is renewed for another cycle. Every time this thin crescent, waxing moon is seen, it signals the first day of a new month. In this way, each month has at least one special day even if it does not have one of the *mo'edim* in it.

Years is an idiom for the seven-year Sabbatical cycle for the land as described in Leviticus 25:1-7, specifically the seventh year. That year was set apart as holy and as rest for the land in a similar way that the Sabbath is distinguished among the days of the week. It is also applied to the year of Jubilee, the year after seven complete cycles of seven years have been completed, as described in Leviticus 25:8-17. It is the year of Jubilee to which Isaiah refers in chapter 61:2 as *"the acceptable year of the LORD "* —quoted by Yeshua in the synagogue in Nazareth.[5]

The 'End Times' according to God's calendar

These four words also carry their usual meanings in Scripture, but just as with English words, they can occasionally convey a cryptic message. In the same way that discovering a subliminal message within those words opens up our eyes to other nuances in the Scriptures, so too will a study of God's calendar. A hobby of

[3] Num. 10:10
[4] This is known as the 'thumbnail of God.'
[5] Luke 4:16-19

mine for over twenty-five years has been to study eschatology—the doctrine of last things. For years I had grappled with the original texts as well as read the conclusions and hypotheses of dozens of authors covering virtually every position on the last days spectrum. While many of them had some good insights and plausible speculations about the time to come and when we could expect events to begin unfolding, I never found one particular view to explain everything sufficiently for me. I ended up with a cross-sectional position composed of individual parts of several doctrines.

When I began to study and read about these *mo'edim*, these appointed times of the LORD, a new and clearer picture emerged from the fog. It is not my intention or purpose to present detailed evidence of their meanings and message; it will suffice for me to say that it is clear that the *mo'edim* are the Messianic agenda. They are the template for God's dealing with man, not only for *what* He has done, is doing and will do, but also *when* He will do it. A simple study of these appointed times will reveal that a high percentage of the major events recorded in the Bible, as well as those of Israel's history, took place on those very dates. God keeps His own calendar; He is not going by the Julian calendar nor the Gregorian one. Our present dating system means nothing to Him. Much of the world held its breath at the arrival of the year 2000, and many Christians were convinced that it had great significance spiritually. They were wrong. Why? Because it was man's date, not God's.

The Template

If we take a look at Passover, probably the most well-known of these *mo'edim*, we can see a glimpse of this template. In the book of Exodus we find the story of this monumental event. God tells Moses to instruct the Israelites living in Egypt to select a lamb or a kid from their flock and slay it on a certain night, then smear some of its blood above and on both sides of their door frame. The blood would then indicate to the angel of death that the occupants of the house belonged to the LORD—bought with the blood of the lamb. The Israelites did what God had instructed them to do, were spared and walked out of Egypt the next day as a free nation.

For centuries after that night, the Jews celebrated Passover in much the same way except for applying the blood around their doors. They thought they were doing it as a remembrance of that night in Egypt; what they were really doing—including that night in Egypt—was rehearsing for the selection and sacrifice of the true Passover Lamb who was to come. He was selected on the 10th of Nisan, just as God had instructed the people to do in Egypt; that is what the procession known as 'the triumphal entry' was all about on 'Palm Sunday.' Then He was killed on the day of Passover, dying as the lambs were being slain in the temple, expiring as the last lamb had been slaughtered. After all the Passover lambs had been killed, the High Priest would proclaim, "It is finished"…and so did Yeshua, our High Priest, declare as the final sacrifice for sin for all time was offered.

It was the same date, the same *mo'ed,* as that night in Egypt. Yet we find another curious entry at Exodus 12:40-41,

> *"Now the sojourn of the children of Israel who lived in Egypt was four hundred and thirty years. And it came to pass at the end of the four hundred and thirty years—**on that very same day**—it came to pass that all the armies of the LORD went out from the land of Egypt."* (emphasis mine)

So we see that another important event had already occurred on this date many years earlier. Coincidence? Rabbi Daniel Lapin doesn't think so:

> "I always thought that Jewish holidays are as a result of certain events which took place in Jewish history. I thought that Pesach (Passover) was because we were taken out of the land of Egypt. The real story is that we

were taken out of Egypt on the fifteenth of Nisan because that was the day which was already preordained as Pesach, long before we associate these one to another. When the angels visited Abraham and Lot, they were given matzos[6] to eat.[7] The rabbinical teaching here believes they were given matzos to eat because it was Pesach, and that Pesach existed long before anybody went into Egypt!"[8]

This same pattern can be demonstrated with each of the *mo'edim* on His schedule. It is the schedule He has kept and will yet keep, as evidenced by details given in the book of Revelation. This is not surprising because in Leviticus 23, the phrase *"it shall be a statute forever throughout your generations"* is connected to the Feasts of Firstfruits (v.14); Weeks, or Pentecost (v. 21); *Yom Kippur,* or the Day of Atonement (v. 31); and *Sukkot,* or the Feast of Tabernacles (v. 41). Back in Exodus 12:14 God had said of Passover, *"You shall keep it as an everlasting ordinance."* Nothing is hinted in these verses about 'keeping or observing them until the Messiah comes.' God obviously knew that He was going to send Messiah in about 1400 years, yet He still said, "Do these forever."

Even though we understand that Messiah 'fulfilled' most of these *mo'edim*, there are yet other appointments booked on these dates. In one of his letters, the apostle Sha'ul encourages the believers by telling them,

> *"So let no one judge you in food or in drink, of regarding a festival or a new moon or a Sabbath, which are a shadow of things to come, the substance is of Messiah."*[9]

He isn't saying, "Don't observe these things;" he's saying, "Don't let anyone judge you for doing them!" He says they are *'a*

---

[6] Unleavened bread
[7] Gen. 19:3
[8] Excerpt from a speech by Rabbi Daniel Lapin about Chanukkah, the Festival of Lights.
[9] Col. 2:16-17

shadow of things to come.' He wrote this long after the resurrection, yet he implies they still have future significance.

Sha'ul himself kept these *mo'edim.* In the book of Acts, Luke recorded that Sha'ul kept the Passover (20:6), Pentecost (20:16), and another unidentified feast (18:21). Sha'ul even gives instructions to the believers in Corinth on how to properly keep Passover.[10]

In the book of Zechariah, he prophesies that after the Messiah sets up His earthly kingdom all nations will go up to Jerusalem every year to celebrate the Feast of Tabernacles, and that those who don't will receive no rain and be struck with a severe plague.[11] Yeshua even alluded to a future Passover when He said to His disciples that night as they ate the Passover meal,

> *"I will not drink this fruit of the vine from now on until that day when I drink it new with you in My Father's kingdom."*[12]

He was referring to the fourth cup of wine, the cup of acceptance,[13] which He will drink with us when He takes us to be His people. It makes no sense to think that He was just talking about wine in general, because He would be killed the following day and, after a brief (40-day) ministry time after His resurrection, He would not be back on earth for many centuries.

We've been robbed!

As I researched these *mo'edim* and became fascinated by the depth of meaning and mystery they hold, I became increasingly aware of a sense of having been robbed for so many years by a

---

[10] 1 Cor. 11:17-34
[11] Zech. 14:16-19
[12] Matt. 26:29
[13] The four cups of the Passover are based on Ex. 6: 6-7: *"I will bring you out..."* (the cup of Sanctification or setting apart); *"I will rescue you..."* (the cup of Deliverance); *"I will redeem you..."* (the cup of Redemption); *"I will take you as My people and I will be your God"* (the cup of Acceptance).

system which had relegated them to the garbage dump of history. I thought to myself, "Why do the holidays of the Church look so much more like the ones of pagan antiquity than the ones God instituted in His Word?" I discovered that it is because the Church thinks of itself as being above and, therefore, having no need for the things of the Old Testament. Speaking of the alleged discontinuity between the Old and New Testaments, Samuelle Bacchiocchi wrote,

> This prevailing view rests on the gratuitous assumption that the coming of Christ brought about a radical discontinuity between the Old and New Testaments, Law and Grace, Judaism and Christianity. The abandonment of the Old Testament Holy Days is seen as the most obvious evidence of this radical discontinuity.
>
> This dualistic and antagonistic understanding of the Old and New Testaments as being mutually exclusive has plagued Christianity during much of its history. It can be traced back to the Gnostic Marcion (about A. D. 150), who rejected the Old Testament and its institutions as products of an evil god. Its influence is still evident today in the dispensational theology, which views Israel and the Church as two separate peoples, with two different origins and destinies.
>
> According to the dispensational construct, the earliest converts who accepted Christ as their Messiah immediately perceived themselves as "the New Israel," with a New Moses, a New Faith and a new liturgical calendar. Supposedly, they immediately recognized that the dispensation of the Law had passed and now they were living in the dispensation of Grace. To give expression to their new faith, the earliest Christians immediately felt the urgency to establish, among other things, new places of worship, namely Christian churches, and new Holy Days, namely Sunday, Easter Sunday, and Christmas.

89

This conception of Christian origins is grossly inaccurate and misleading. The New Testament recognizes that Christ's coming brought about a certain discontinuity by fulfilling Old Testament typological institutions, but this discontinuity is never interpreted in terms of abrogation of the Mosaic law, in general, or of Holy Days, in particular.[14]

By now you have learned that the early believers did, in fact, keep the appointed times on God's calendar. You may also have picked up on the fact that as Gentiles began to outnumber the Jews in the congregations, a gradual shift took place in the way the believers expressed their faith. This was also due, in part, to the deaths of the apostles and their successors; i.e., they were no longer around to keep correcting doctrinal errors.

By the middle of the second century C.E., virtually the entire Church—especially the leadership—were of non-Jewish origin. Some of the so-called 'Church fathers' were vehemently anti-Semitic: Justin Martyr and Origen were both highly respected churchmen and eloquently attacked the Jews and incited the believers against them.

The posture of the Church was decisively set against the Synagogue. Whereas one gentile nation after another had responded positively to the Christian missionary outreach, the Synagogue continued to cling stubbornly to its ancestral faith, leaving the Church increasingly frustrated and embittered. Sermons, dialogues, diatribes, and polemics became the order of the day. [15]

Near the beginning of the fourth century C.E., Constantine became the Roman Emperor. Early in his reign he claimed to have had a vision of a cross in the sky and heard the words, "In

---

[14] Bacchiocchi, Samuelle, *God's Festivals in Scripture and History, Part 1—The Spring Festivals;* (Berrien Springs, Biblical Perspectives, 1995), p. 84-85
[15] Wilson, Marvin R., *Our Father Abraham*, p. 92

this sign conquer." He was motivated to 'convert to Christianity'[16] by this experience and declared Christianity to be the new state religion. This was a relief to the believers, but it was the beginning of another wave of persecution and hatred toward the Jews.

In 325 C.E., Constantine convened the first ecumenical Council in Nicea for the purpose of establishing common doctrine within the Church. One of the best-known products of this Council is the Nicene Creed. What is *not* commonly known is that there were other decrees made by this Council that would forever change the face of Christianity.

The first of these is that the day of worship was officially changed to Sunday. Most Gentile churches had already adopted this day as an act of disassociation from the Jews, but now it was enforced as dogma, and the penalty upon any who continued to observe the Jewish Sabbath was excommunication from the Church. Sunday had already come to be called 'the Lord's Day' or 'Imperial Day,' not in honour of Yeshua, but in honour of the Roman Emperor.[17]

Secondly, believers were forbidden to observe 'the Jewish festivals' because the Council stated that Messiah had made them obsolete and void of meaning. One of the primary reasons this council was convened was to settle the dispute over 'the proper day of keeping Easter, some celebrating the festival in the manner of the Jews and others following the customs of Christians throughout the rest of the world.'[18]

This shows how great a gulf had come between the Christians and the Jews, for Jews did not (and do not) celebrate Easter. Easter is the festival in honour of the goddess Easter (a.k.a. Ishtar, Isis, Aphrodite, et al.) who is the goddess of fertility. Her worshippers venerated her in symbols such as eggs and rabbits. The celebration of the spring fertility rite predates the time of

---

[16] History attests that this was a purely politically-motivated gesture, and that he remained a sun worshipper until his death.

[17] *The New Standard Jewish Encyclopedia,* pg. 214 (see also chapter 3 on the Sabbath)

[18] *Eusebius' Ecclesiastical History* (Peabody, Hendrickson Publishers, 1998), p. 390

Yeshua by many centuries. Further evidence is seen when early Church historian Eusebius records,

> It appears the churches of Syria and Mesopotamia continued to follow the custom of the Jews and celebrated Easter on the fourteenth day of the moon, whether falling on Sunday or not. All the other churches observed that solemnity on Sunday only, namely, those of Rome, Italy, Africa, Lybia, Egypt, Spain, Gaul, and Britain; and all Greece, Asia and Pontus.[19]

This shows clearly that *they were confusing Easter with Passover*. No wonder there was such controversy! Even if 'Easter Sunday' coincides with the feast of Firstfruits—the day Yeshua rose again—it, i.e., Firstfruits, can *never* coincide with Passover for the following reason: Leviticus 23:5 plainly states that Passover is the 14th of Nisan. Verse 6 says that the feast of Unleavened Bread begins the next day and lasts for seven days. Then in verse 11 the day of Firstfruits is decreed to occur on "*the day after the Sabbath*." Passover and Unleavened Bread are fixed dates, but *Firstfruits is a fixed day of the week*—the first day. Firstfruits always falls on the day after the Sabbath in the week of Unleavened Bread. If Passover (Nisan 14th) were to fall on the first day of the week (Sunday), Firstfruits would be the following Sunday (Nisan 21st). If Passover falls on Friday, Firstfruits would be two days later (Nisan 16th).

These non-Jewish believers were trying to celebrate Yeshua's resurrection on the day He was crucified—i.e., Passover! The Council rightly made a distinction between the two days, but fixed the method of determining Easter as the first Sunday after the first full moon after the vernal equinox.[20] Some years this method works, others it is a month off. Had they at least stuck with the Sunday after Passover, they would have been correct every year. The Christian system is also faulty in its perpetual

---

[19] ibid. p. 400
[20] This was calculated so that Passover and Easter could never coincide.

distinguishing of 'Good Friday' as the day of the crucifixion. As I showed above, Passover can occur on any day of the week, not just Friday, and we *can* be sure of the date of the crucifixion.

Anchors Aweigh!

With their Jewish foundation now totally abandoned by the Church, the doors were open for whatever someone wanted to bring in and incorporate into the cycle of worship. There was no longer a biblical standard to direct the observance of Holy Days, or even to dictate the Holy Days to be observed. Soon after the Council of Nicea, Christianity adopted another holiday.

> The festival of Christmas became a regular practice in the West about the middle of the fourth century, with the adoption of the December date that had been previously used by the pagans.[21]

Again it is noted that this festival had been in existence for some time previous to the birth of Yeshua. It was known to the Romans as Saturnalia and was a celebration of the rebirth of the sun. The basic story is that each year the sun becomes less and less powerful and is thought to 'die' on the winter solstice of December 21/22. After three days, when it is 'resurrected' as evidenced by its strength noticeably increasing, a festival was held to *Sol Invictus*—the unconquered sun. This is the reason for the December 25th date. This date was also known as the birthday of the Roman sun-god Zeus, which is why Antiochus Epiphanes IV sacrificed a pig on the altar of the Jewish temple in Jerusalem on December 25th of 168 B.C.E.

These are just a couple of examples of the holidays that are esteemed and propagated by the Church. With little effort we can determine that they are nothing but secular days, set apart for

---

[21] Cairns, Earle E.; *Christianity Through the Centuries* (Grand Rapids, Zondervan, 1954), p. 160

worshipping false gods, deceptively covered with a coat of 'Christian paint' so they are acceptable. In this sense they are very much like the infamous Trojan horse that the citizens of Troy accepted as a gift of peace but that brought death in its belly.

"But that's not what it means to ME!"

The common response by Christians to the questionable origins of these holidays is "Now we celebrate the birth/resurrection of Jesus on those days, not the pagan meanings." I wish I could say that were true, for although they may say that, we must look at the practices which accompany the days before we can arrive at a verdict.

- If Easter is solely a day to commemorate the resurrection, why do so many churches have Easter egg hunts for the children or give out chocolate rabbits?
- If Christmas is the day to commemorate Jesus' birth, why the tree, the wreaths and the gifts?
- Perhaps raising more suspicion than both of the above is the question, if these are really days to worship God and exalt Jesus, why does the non-believing world join with such abandon?

The answer is that these holidays belonged to the non-believers to begin with and the Church adopted those days to attract the non-believers in the door. The message to the unsaved was clear: you don't have to change what you are doing; just come to church and it will be all right.

I also can't help but notice that the secular world isn't the least bit interested in Passover, Pentecost or the Feast of Tabernacles. It is only recently that a minority *within* the Church has become interested in learning about them. The truth is that if we follow God's calendar of appointed times, we will celebrate all of the events on the Messianic agenda:

- His birth – Tabernacles;
- His death – Passover;
- His burial – Unleavened Bread;

- His resurrection – Firstfruits;
- His outpouring of the Holy Spirit – Pentecost;
- His return for His bride – Trumpets;
- Judgment Day – Yom Kippur;
- His return to earth – Tabernacles; and
- the establishment of His kingdom on earth – Sabbath.

It is a major accomplishment of Satan to derail believers from the track God set out. God said these are His appointments; He shows up to every one, but the people who claim to know Him so well continue to 'stand Him up' week after week, year after year, appointment after appointment. They show up on other days, expecting Him to be there.

Some bad examples

1. Aaron had a little calf…

We have some examples in the Bible that parallel the circumstances and situations within the Church today and for the last nineteen hundred years. The first is found in Exodus 32.

> *Now when the people saw that Moses delayed coming down from the mountain, the people gathered together to Aaron, and said to him, "Come, make us gods that shall go before us; for as for this Moses, the man who brought us up out of the land of Egypt, we do not know what has become of him."*
> *And Aaron said to them, "Break off the golden earrings which are in the ears of your wives, your sons, and your daughters, and bring them to me." So all the people broke off the golden earrings which were in their ears, and brought them to Aaron. And he received the gold from their hand, and he fashioned it with an engraving tool, and made a molded calf.*

95

> *Then they said, "This is your god, O Israel, that brought you out of the land of Egypt!"*
>
> *So when Aaron saw it, he built an altar before it. And Aaron made a proclamation and said, " Tomorrow is a feast to the LORD." Then they rose early on the next day, offered burnt offerings, and brought peace offerings; and the people sat down to eat and drink, and rose up to play.*
>
> *And the LORD said to Moses, "Go, get down! For your people whom you brought up out of the land of Egypt have corrupted themselves. They have turned aside quickly out of the way which I commanded them."*[22]

Moses delayed coming down from the mountain and the people got impatient and bored; they wanted some action, some fun. Aaron, the authority figure in Moses' absence, acquiesced to their whims and whipped up a quick little calf to suit the purpose. But he did two things even worse than that:

1. He let the people call it by the name of God, the eternal One, and
2. He declared, *"Tomorrow is a feast* [mo'ed] *to the* LORD*."*

Now we might think that God would have been honoured by His people's affection for Him, that they couldn't wait for Moses to come back to get the party going. After all, isn't that what Moses had told Pharaoh they were going into the desert to do?

> *Afterward, Moses and Aaron went in and told Pharaoh, "Thus says the LORD God of Israel: 'Let My people go that they may hold a feast to Me in the wilderness.'"*[23]

However, God wasn't touched by this gesture; He was ticked! He told Moses to stand aside while He incinerated the whole bunch of them. It was a proof of Moses' heart for the people that

---

[22] Ex. 32:1-8a
[23] Ex. 5:1

he didn't budge but actually stood in God's sights so He wouldn't destroy them. I find it amusing in their dialogue that God calls Israel *"your people whom you have brought up out of the land of Egypt"* and Moses calls them *"Your people whom You have brought up out of the land of Egypt."* Neither one of them wanted to claim Israel at that moment.

The people didn't expect Moses to be gone so long; some of them even thought he might not come back. Similarly, the early believers thought Yeshua would return within their lifetimes. Even the apostle Sha'ul appears not to have been let in on the '2000-year delay' detail. Once the believers clued in that it may be awhile before He returns, they 'turned from the way' and created other ways to represent Yeshua. Israel used the Egyptian bull deity as their model; Christianity uses the pagan fertility goddess and sun god as theirs, even declaring the days of those gods to be celebrations—feasts, complete with ham—to God the Sun, I mean Son. Do I think He is any more pleased or more tolerant today than that day so long ago? Not at all. I'm sure it is only by Moses'—I mean Messiah's—intercession that we have been spared from the wrath of God.

What was it about Israel's actions on that day that made God so angry, angry to the point that He considered annihilating the nation He had just brought to birth? They had taken a heathen god, called it by His name and began to worship it as the Egyptians had done, even declaring a holy day for the purpose.

A jealous God

One of the adjectives God uses to describe Himself is 'jealous.'[24] We usually confuse jealousy with envy, which is a feeling we have toward someone else about the way they are—their looks, personality, etc.—or what they have. The Hebrew concept of jealousy is one of wanting what you should have because it is yours. It is an attitude that is *for* someone rather than

---

[24] E.g., Ex. 20:5; 34:14; Dt. 4:24, et al. In Ex 34:14, God even says that His name *is* Jealous!

of someone, as in 'a man is jealous for his wife because she is rightfully his.' That is how God is about His people and His name. They belong to Him and He will act to protect them just as any good husband would act to protect his wife. However, when His people are the ones who are guilty of profaning His name and His 'reputation,' then He will act against them to vindicate His holy name. This includes any form of idolatry that displaces God from His rightful place of pre-eminence. The references in Exodus 20:5 and Deuteronomy 4:24 are both in the context of warning against making images for worship, exactly what Israel had done while Moses was still up on Mt. Sinai.

God gave them clear directions in Leviticus 18:3 not to do the things that were done in the land of Egypt from where they had been delivered, nor to do the things that were done in the land of Canaan where they were going. He wants His people to be different, holy, set apart from the world, and that only happens when they obey His will. Moses also gave them a stern warning in His final address to the nation:

> *"When the LORD your God cuts off from before you the nations which you go to dispossess, and you displace them and dwell in their land, take heed to yourself that you are not ensnared to follow them, after they are destroyed from before you, and that you do not inquire after their gods, saying, 'How did these nations serve their gods? I also will do likewise.'* **You shall not worship the LORD your God in that way.**"[25] (emphasis mine)

He said, in essence, "Don't adopt something which those heathen people do to worship their gods and then say you are worshipping the LORD." In the final analysis, it comes down to this: we can only worship God in the way that He has ordained; anything else is despicable to Him regardless of how good it makes us feel. (It sounds like the Israelites were enjoying themselves on their self-proclaimed holy day, too.)

---

[25] Dt. 12:29-31a

History repeats itself

Despite all the warnings and the near-fatal disaster with the golden calf, eventually Israel drifted back into the forbidden realm of idolatry. Solomon had gotten the 'idolatry ball' rolling while he was king of Israel. It began with all his foreign wives who turned his heart away from the LORD. He fell so deep into idolatry that he built places of worship to some of these false gods, so much so that the Mount of Olives became known as the Mount of Corruption.[26] After Solomon's death the kingdom was split in two; ten tribes seceded under the leadership of Jeroboam[27], and two tribes remained faithful to Solomon's son Rehoboam. (Why did it have to be two guys with similar-sounding names?)

Even though Jeroboam got 80% of the nation, he didn't get Jerusalem, which, of course, was where the temple was. Soon into his kingship, 'Jerry' figured out that if the people of his kingdom were still going to be going to Jerusalem to offer sacrifices (which they were), eventually they would decide to go back on Rehoboam's side. His solution? He made two gold calves and said to the people,

> *"Here are your gods, O Israel, which brought you up from the land of Egypt!"*[28]

Does this sound vaguely familiar to you? He set one up in a city he established and called Bethel, (meaning *the house of God*, but not the same place where Jacob had had his dream[29]); the other he put 'in Dan,' i.e., in the portion of land allotted to the tribe of Dan.

Next, he ordained priests from among the people who were not even Levites, let alone descendants of Aaron.[30] As an

---

[26] 2 Kings 23:13
[27] Jeroboam was from the tribe of Ephraim (1 Kings 11:26)
[28] 1 Kings 12:28
[29] That Bethel later became Jerusalem, specifically the Temple Mount.
[30] 1 Kings 12:31

ultimate act of replacement theology, he declared a feast—a
mo'ed—

> *"on the 15th day of the eighth month, like the feast that*
> *was in Judah...in the month which he devised in his own*
> *heart."*[31]

Jeroboam's sin was the introduction and propagation of a
form of worship of his own design to replace that which God
Himself had commanded. Don't think that Jeroboam wasn't
well aware of what he was doing or that the similarities to the
other golden calf incident were mere coincidences. He even
named his sons Nadab[32] and Abiyah[33] like Aaron's two sons
who were killed by the LORD for offering strange fire in the
tabernacle.[34]

In the Church today, this sin of Jeroboam is alive and
well:

- The focus for direction and instruction has been
  shifted from Jerusalem to a man-established city—the
  Vatican City in Rome.
- God's calendar has been discarded and replaced with
  the pagan calendar, thus obscuring the Messianic
  agenda for man's redemption. Days such as Easter,
  Christmas and even Mother's Day and Valentine's Day
  are observed with sentimental sermons, rather than
  God's holy days being observed.
- Pagan practices are brought in to the Church under the
  guise of worship. Even symbols representing pagan
  deities are brought into the sanctuary and members'
  homes. (If you don't think that a Christmas tree—
  described in Jeremiah 10:1-5—is an idol, just try to get
  rid of it![35])

---

[31] 1 Kings 12:32-33
[32] 1 Kings 14:20
[33] 1 Kings 14:1
[34] Lev. 10:1-2
[35] I did this one year at the church I was pastoring; I thought it was an interesting
'coincidence' that I was asked to resign at the end of November the following year.

Choosing the right assembly

I challenge you to investigate for yourself the origins of the holidays you keep. Whether or not it is how or why you keep the day is immaterial; the origins have set the course. God gave specific instructions about specific days, days that He has marked on His calendar to interface with man. If the enemy of our souls can keep us confused about those times or, worse, convinced that they are bondage to us and detrimental to our spiritual 'freedom,' then the chances of us ever meeting the Almighty at an appointed time are very remote.

The writer of Hebrews was aware of Satan's efforts to disrupt these occasions to connect with God; he wrote,

> *And let us consider one another in order to stir up love and good works, not forsaking the assembling of ourselves together as is the manner of some, but exhorting one another, and so much the more as you see the Day approaching.*[36]

The 'assembling of ourselves together' to which he refers is not 'church on Sunday morning.' Instead, he is referring to the holy convocations which the LORD has instituted as His appointed times.

Consider the holidays you keep; they reveal the god you serve.

---

[36] Heb. 10:24-25

Part Two

Torah or Not Torah?

That Is the Question

Chapter 6

What Torah Is and Is Not

I didn't feel that this book would be complete without an explanation of what I see as an alternative to the typical Christian lifestyle. If you have read this far and been able to keep an open heart and mind to the evidence I've presented, you may be slightly disenchanted with 'the faith' you have cherished for such a long time. I want to point out as I did in the opening chapter, that these departures from the clear teaching of Scripture are due to human influence rather than 'new revelation' from God through Yeshua. The solution to the problem of incorrect doctrine and direction in the life of a believer has been in your hands all along...you just never knew it. You have probably been warned against it by well-meaning friends and pastors, and so I am going to present this last bit of evidence for you to evaluate. It goes beyond just identification, beyond Sabbath; it affects every area of your life. It is the *Torah*, the instructions of God to mankind, given within the first five books of the Bible. You may know this body of teaching as 'the Law;' if you do, then you don't know what it contains.

Throughout my Christian life, I never once considered that there was any validity or relevance to my life within those books. They were stories of the great patriarchs and the founding of the nation of Israel, with little that could affect me today. The Law was a code for conduct that continually proved my inability to measure up to God's standard. I was told it was given to show how hopelessly sinful we humans really are, and that God, in His mercy, buried it forever when Yeshua was crucified...but then I took a look at it for myself.

One day several years ago, we met a Messianic couple at a church we were attending. We didn't know they were Messianic at the time, and looking back on it now, we think they were placed there by God for our sakes. They were only at the church for a short time before moving on, but during that time they would ask us questions that made me uncomfortable...because I couldn't answer them. Of all the difficult questions they asked, the one which eventually led to my opening the door to consider something other than 'the party line' was this: "If God set the Jews aside because they were disobedient to His law and broke His covenant, why did He then turn to the Gentiles and say, in effect, 'You don't have to worry about it.' Why didn't He just say to Israel, 'You know what? Let's just scrap this whole thing and start over. It was a bad idea from the start.' "

So I began to search the Scriptures for the reasons why the Gentiles were exempt from 'the bondage of the Law.' It was one of those cases of finding something I never expected.

In the previous chapters I have described how Yeshua lived and taught the *Torah*, and how the Sabbath and the festivals—all instituted within the *Torah*—still have significance today. In this chapter I want to share with you some of the discoveries I made about the message in the Bible—the whole Bible—of the absolute importance of living according to the *Torah*.

When we approach the Bible to search out objective truth, it is imperative that we start with a 'blank page;' we must set aside all of our predrawn conclusions and our preconceived ideas. If we begin with the same premises we have always begun with, we will arrive at the same conclusions we have always arrived at.

Word Definitions from the 'Bible' Dictionary

"Effective communication requires an understanding of common words and ideas exchanged between people. Without that understanding, communication can be reduced to babble. The same is true in Bible study. Although the words of the Bible are ancient, relative to our present time, they nonetheless must be understood in their original language and context. In short, a mistake oftentimes made in religious circles today is to redefine words and concepts from first-century Judaism. We can see this in all things from classroom curriculum to new Bible translations to speaking and teaching others about the Messiah and His work. Wrong comprehension of ancient biblical words and ideas can naturally lead us to unwittingly propagate untruthfulness about God, His Mashiach and His Message."[1]

In order to understand what the writers of the New Testament (the only part of the Bible most Christians think has any bearing on their life today) meant when they wrote, we must discover what the words they used meant to them. If we define New Testament words such as righteousness, faith, freedom, light, grace, truth, etc., by what we deduce from the New Testament, we are guilty of circular reasoning. In order for us to understand what Yeshua and the apostles meant by these terms, we must discover their meaning in the same 'dictionary' they used: the *Tanakh*[2]—what you know as the 'Old Testament.'

Torah

The word *Torah* can be generally applied to the first five books of the Bible, also known as 'the Law' or 'the Pentateuch,' but the manner in which I will use it here is as it is literally defined: 'teaching' or 'instruction.' It is the directions for living that are contained in the books of Exodus through Deuteronomy. In Hebrew, *Torah* is a four-letter word, and I think to many people it is a four-letter word in English as well.

The root word of *torah* is *yara*, which means 'to throw, to shoot or to teach.' The idea is that *Torah* is like an arrow shot from a bow that is meant to hit the mark or the target. When a teacher teaches, his words are 'targeted' at his audience. The concept resulted in the idea that if one followed the words of the teacher he would hit the mark or reach the goal. We can see this principle at work today when a person who plays tennis or golf hires a personal coach to improve his game, or when a business

---

[1] Avi ben Mordechai , *Messiah, Volume 1: Understanding His life and Teachings in Hebraic Context* (Millennium 7000, 1997), p. 79

[2] *Tanakh* is an acronym for the three parts of the Hebrew Scriptures: *Torah* (the five books of Moses), *Nevi'im* (the Prophets) and the *Ketuvim* (the writings).

hires a consultant to improve its bottom line. The hope is that the instruction will help them reach their goal.

To the ancient Israelites and the Patriarchs before them, the words of *Torah*—the instructions—were so vital to living that several other phrases emerged in their vocabulary as euphemisms for '*Torah*.'

1. Righteousness

The definition of righteousness I was taught as a boy in Sunday school is 'right-standing with God.' This definition is indeed a true explanation of righteousness, but unfortunately needs definition itself as to what 'right-standing' implies. Moses gives us a clearer explanation in the book of Deuteronomy. He said,

> *"When your son asks you in time to come, saying, 'What is the meaning of the testimonies, the statutes and the judgments which the LORD our God has commanded you?' then you shall say to your son, 'We were slaves of Pharaoh in Egypt, and the LORD brought us out of Egypt with a mighty hand; and the LORD showed signs and wonders before our eyes, great and severe, against Egypt, Pharaoh, and all his household. Then He brought us out from there, that He might bring us in, to give us the land of which He swore to our fathers. And the LORD commanded us to observe all these statutes, to fear the LORD our God for our good always, that He might preserve us alive, as it is this day. **Then it will be righteousness for us, if we are careful to observe all these commandments before the LORD our God, as He has commanded us.**'"* [3](emphasis mine)

The implication we are given here is that righteousness = following the instructions, i.e., the commandments of God. This

---

[3] Deut. 6:20-25

understanding is reflected in the writings of David. In the 119th Psalm he wrote,

> *"My tongue shall speak of your word,*
> *For all your commandments are righteousness."*[4]

The idea that righteousness is not just a quality that is imputed to us, but rather something to be pursued or followed, is conveyed in the 23rd Psalm where he wrote,

> *"He leads me in **the paths of righteousness**, for His name's sake."*[5]

A path is a pre-determined track for travelling between two places. It is not as though He has left us to wander aimlessly without direction in this wilderness we call 'the world;' He has set the path and marked it clearly so we cannot miss the trail. Originally it was a well-worn track, but then gradually it was used less and less as His people *"turned everyone to his own way,"*[6] as Isaiah put it. When Messiah arrived on earth, He found the trail overgrown with thorns and weeds; men had fallen trees across the path to hinder any who would venture to walk that way. He came and cleared all the debris and obstacles from the path of righteousness so we could once again see the way.

The Prophet Ezekiel was given a message for Israel to encourage them to repentance. Through him, the LORD said,

> *"But if a man is **just** [same word as 'righteous']*
> *And does what is lawful and right;*
> *If he has not eaten on the mountains,*
> *Nor lifted up his eyes to the idols of the house of Israel,*
> *Nor defiled his neighbour's wife,*
> *Nor approached a woman during her impurity;*

---

[4] Ps. 119:172
[5] Ps. 23:3
[6] Is. 53:6

If he has not oppressed anyone,
But has restored to the debtor his pledge;
Has robbed no one by violence,
But has given his bread to the hungry
And covered the naked with clothing;
If he has not exacted usury
Nor taken any increase,
But has withdrawn his hand from iniquity
And executed true judgment between man and man;
If he has walked in My statutes
And kept My judgments faithfully –
He is just; [righteous]
He shall surely live!"
Says the LORD God.[7] (emphasis mine)

Later in that same chapter the LORD said,

"But if a wicked man turns from all his sins which he has committed, keeps all My statutes, and does what is lawful and right, he shall surely live; he shall not die. None of the transgressions which he has committed shall be remembered against him; ***because of the righteousness which he has done,*** *he shall live."* [8](emphasis mine)

Again, righteousness is seen as the result of a choice of lifestyle, that of following the statutes and judgments of the LORD. It is worth noting that also in this eighteenth chapter of Ezekiel can be found the definition of 'repentance' when the LORD says,

Again, when a wicked man ***turns away*** *from the wickedness which he committed and does what is lawful and right, he preserves himself alive...****Repent****, and turn from all your transgressions, so that iniquity will not be*

---

[7] Ezk. 18:5-9
[8] Ezk. 18:21-22

110

your ruin.[9] (emphasis mine)

The words 'turn away' and 'repent' are the same Hebrew word. It is fairly common knowledge within Christianity that repentance means to 'turn around' from the direction you are going, but what is not well known is that true repentance is when you turn from your way of sin and turn to what is lawful and right (literally, 'justice and righteousness'), i.e., do what the *Torah* directs.

2. Life

Moses gives us another analogy for the blessings of following the instructions of the LORD that also ties in with the message by Ezekiel. Moses said,

> *"Set your hearts on all the words which I testify among you today, which you shall command your children to be careful to observe—all the words of this law* [Torah]. *For it is not a futile thing for you, because* ***it is your life,*** *and by this word you shall prolong your days in the land which you cross over the Jordan to possess."*[10] (emphasis mine)

Moses was very emphatic in his declaration to the people that following the words of 'this law' would be life for them, i.e., doing so would increase the length of the days they would live as well as the quality of those days.

David makes allusion to 'life' being something to be walked in when he said,

> *"You will show me* ***the path of life;*** *in your presence is fullness of joy; at your right hand are pleasures*

---

forevermore."[11] (emphasis mine)

Solomon also understood it that way, for he wrote,

He who keeps instruction is in the way of life, but he who refuses correction goes astray.[12]

The only instructions that will give life are the ones Moses relayed to the people from the LORD while they were in the wilderness.

3. 'The Way of the LORD,' or just 'The Way'

In the above quote from Proverbs, Solomon used this metaphor that was also commonly employed to mean the *Torah*. We see the first instance of it in a conversation between the LORD and Moses at the time of the 'golden calf incident.' The LORD said,

*"Go, get down! For your people whom you brought out of the land of Egypt have corrupted themselves. They have turned aside quickly out of **the way** which I commanded them.*"[13] (emphasis mine)

Here the LORD gives positive identification to 'the way' by describing it as "[the one which] *I have commanded them.*" Once again, we see this same thought echoed by David in his songs. He wrote,

Blessed are the undefiled in the way,
Who walk in the law [Torah] *of the LORD!*
Blessed are those who keep His testimonies,
Who seek Him with their whole heart!

---

[11] Ps. 16:11
[12] Pr. 10:17
[13] Ex. 32:7-8b

They also do no iniquity.
They walk in His ways.[14]

The message is also conveyed in these verses, which appear in my Bible like this:

The steps of a good man are ordered by the LORD,
And He delights in his way.
Though he fall, he shall not be utterly cast down;
For the LORD upholds him with His hand.[15]

However, since there are no capital letters in Hebrew, this meaning is the result of the translator's bias. I believe the first verse should read like this:

The steps of a good man are ordered by the LORD,
And he delights in His way.

By simply reversing the capitalized 'He' in the sentence, the meaning is totally changed. In the first quotation, it is implied that the LORD is pleased with the way that a good man has chosen to walk. I have no problem with that, but it doesn't explain what direction it is the good man is walking (although we can assume it is good since the man is called 'good'). In the second quotation it is clear that the man is walking in 'His way,' i.e., the way of the LORD. Not only is that man *walking* in the way of the LORD, but he *delights* in it. Reading it this way also clarifies the beginning half of the sentence; the 'steps' that are 'ordered' are the instructions—the path—that the LORD has laid out for a man to walk in.

The prophet Jeremiah delivered a message from the LORD to the kingdom of Judah that explained why disaster was coming upon them (just in case they couldn't figure it out):

---

[14] Ps. 119:1-3
[15] Ps. 37:23-24

Thus says the LORD:
"Stand in the ways and see,
*And ask for the old paths, where **the good way** is,*
And walk in it;
Then you will find rest for your souls.
But they said, 'We will not walk in it.'
Also I set watchmen over you, saying,
'Listen to the sound of the trumpet!'
But they said, 'We will not listen.'
Therefore hear, you nations,
And know, O congregation, what is among them,
Hear O earth!
Behold I will certainly bring calamity upon this people—
The fruit of their thoughts,
Because they have not heeded My words
Nor my law, but rejected it. "[16]

It is worth noting that in this passage are the words Yeshua said in Matt. 11:29—*"And you shall find rest for your souls."* He was quoting Jeremiah, referring to the rest and peace one finds when one walks in the 'old paths,' i.e., the *Torah*.

In Yeshua's day, people didn't own their own copy of the Scriptures; there was usually only one copy in town, in the synagogue. For that reason, people committed much of the Scriptures to memory. (That was also way before the division of the Bible into chapters and verses, so they would just say, "In the book of Jeremiah..." to identify the passage.) When a teacher would quote from the *Tanakh*, immediately those who knew the passage would know the context surrounding it and make the full connection with the teacher's point. In quoting this line from this context in Jeremiah, Yeshua was equating His yoke and His burden with the old paths—the *Torah*; that is the only way He could give them rest.

---

[16] Jer. 6:16-19

4. The Word of the LORD

We see this euphemism used for the *Torah* in Numbers 15:30-31. The LORD is explaining to Israel how serious an offence it is to wilfully and presumptuously disregard His instructions:

> *"But the person who does anything presumptuously, whether he is native-born or a stranger, that one brings reproach on the LORD, and he shall be cut off from among his people. Because he has despised **the word of the LORD**, and has broken **His commandment**, that person shall be completely cut off; his guilt shall be upon him."*
> (emphasis mine)

We see it again in Deuteronomy 4:1-2;

> *"Now, O Israel, listen to the statutes and the judgments which I teach you to observe, that you may live, and go in and possess the land which the LORD God of your fathers is giving you. You shall not add to **the word which I command you**, nor take from it, that you may keep the commandments of the LORD your God which I command you."*

A common way for Hebrew writers in the Bible to express their point is to use a method known as a 'doublet.' A doublet is when a writer or speaker says the same thing twice in a row but using different words. This is done for clarity and emphasis of the thought conveyed. There are hundreds of examples of this in the Bible, and when the reader recognizes them, he can discover many other euphemisms for common words. In the following two quotations you will see examples of doublets that definitely connect 'the word of the LORD' to the *Torah*.

He declares His word to Jacob;
His statutes and His judgments to Israel.[17]

Here the psalmist equates 'His word' with 'His statutes and judgments,' and 'Jacob' corresponds to 'Israel.'

Isaiah makes an equally revealing statement in the second chapter of his book:

Many people shall come and say,
"Come, and let us go up to the mountain of the LORD,
To the house of the God of Jacob;
He will teach us His ways,
And we shall walk in His paths."
For out of Zion shall go forth the law,
The word of the LORD from Jerusalem.[18]

Here we have four doublets:
1. the mountain of the LORD = the house of the God of Jacob
2. His ways = His paths
3. Zion = Jerusalem, and
4. The law = the word of the LORD

He also made a similar one in the first chapter:

Hear the word of the LORD,
You rulers of Sodom;
Give ear to the law of our God,
You people of Gommorah.[19]

He was not saying two different things to the two cities; he only has one message to deliver.

We can gain new insight into some other expressions from the

---

[17] Ps. 147:19
[18] Is. 2:3
[19] Is. 1:10

Tanakh when we know the proper definition of these terms. For example, the popular Sunday school memory verses and songs taken from David's writings have a whole new meaning:

> *Thy word is a lamp unto my feet, and a light unto my path*[20]

And,

> *Thy word have I hidden in my heart, that I might not sin against Thee.*[21] (We will touch on the definition of sin when we get into the teachings of Yeshua and the apostles.)

5. The Will of God

In thinking about the concept of the will of God, it is logical and correct to believe that His will is what He wants us to do. Therefore responding to His will in a positive way would be considered obedience. For years I, like many Christians, strove to discover His will for my life; I prayed, "God, what do you want me to do?" I had been taught that there was an individual will of God for me that I must find or else I would be walking in disobedience.

Even before I became a Messianic believer, I came across a book called *Decision Making and the Will of God* by Garry Friesen in which the author debunked that myth for me. His basic conclusion is that the will of God is a one-size-fits-all commission and that it is contained within the Scriptures. Today, my only problem with the book is that he didn't recognize the teachings of the Old Testament as having validity for the modern Christian. Yes, God occasionally wants some of us to do things that others won't be required to do, but in cases like that He will communicate those instructions to us directly through objective methods such as dreams, visions, or words of knowledge, not subjectively through impressions, feelings, or a sense of 'peace.'

---

[20] Ps. 119:105
[21] Ps. 119:11

In Psalm 40:8 we have a clear connection of the will of God to the *Torah*.

> *"I delight to do Your will, O my God;*
> *Your law* [Torah] *is within my heart."*

We have a friend who grew up in a very legalistic church as a child. When she began to hear the truth of *Torah*, she told us that all her life she had been seeking to find God's will, and on many occasions had remarked "Why didn't He just write it down for us so it wouldn't be so hard to figure out?" Now she says she's discovered that He *did* write it down for us. There is such peace in knowing beyond a doubt whether or not you are walking in the will of God. No more trying to find the 'needle in the haystack' or the 'dot in the centre of the target;' just trying to decide if you will do it or not.

6. [The] Truth

The biblical usage of the Hebrew word *emet* which means 'truth or faithfulness' is used in several contexts, but all of which relate to God directly or indirectly. It is a character of God's nature, and is fittingly applied to His words.

> As we study it [the word *emet*] in its various contexts, it becomes manifestly clear that there is no truth in the biblical sense, i.e., valid truth, outside God. All truth comes from God and is truth because it is related to God.[22]

Truth, as the ancient Hebrews understood it, was something that they could rely upon, something firm and unmoveable. By the time Israel was established in the Promised Land, the *Torah* was described with the term 'truth' or 'the truth.' This does not imply that the word 'truth' only applied to the *Torah*, but indirectly the *Torah* provided that backdrop against which all

---

[22] *Theological Wordbook of the Old Testament*, p. 116

truth was measured for veracity. Something was 'truth' or considered 'true' if it was as trustworthy as the *Torah*. The psalmists and the prophets repeatedly used the word 'truth' as a euphemism for the *Torah*. The following examples are just a few of the many occurrences of this substitution:

*Show me Your **ways**, O LORD,*
*Teach me Your **paths**.*
*Lead me in Your **truth** and teach me,*
For You are the God of my salvation;
On You I wait all the day.[23]

Your righteousness is an everlasting righteousness,
*And **Your law** [Heb. Torah] **is truth**.*[24]

You are near, O LORD,
*And **all Your commandments are truth**.*[25]

Speaking to the corrupt priests of Israel, the LORD said;

"Behold I will rebuke your descendants and spread refuse on your faces, the refuse of your solemn feasts; and one will take you away with it.
Then you shall know that I have sent this commandment to you, that My covenant with Levi may continue,"
Says the LORD of Hosts.
"My covenant was with him, one of life and peace,
And I gave them to him that he might fear Me;
So he feared Me and was reverent before My name.
***The law** [Heb. Torah] **of truth was in his mouth**, and injustice was not found on his lips.*
He walked with Me in peace and equity, and turned many away from iniquity.

---

[23] Ps. 25:4-5
[24] Ps. 119. 142
[25] Ps. 119:151

For the lips of a priest should keep knowledge,
And people should seek the law [Heb. Torah] *from his*
mouth; for he is the messenger of the LORD of Hosts.
But you have departed from the way;
You have caused many to stumble at the law [Heb. Torah],
You have corrupted the covenant of Levi,"
Says the LORD of hosts.[26]

What Torah is NOT

There are many other idioms and euphemisms in the Bible for the *Torah*, but these are the main ones that appear in the New Testament with great regularity. For now I would like to spend some time clearing some confusion regarding what the *Torah* is not.

1. Bondage

There is a common position held by Christianity—based, they say, on the teachings of Yeshua and Sha'ul—that Yeshua came to set us free (☺) from the bondage of the law (☹). Something about the word 'law' makes us recoil in disgust; the word definitely is loaded with negative connotations. So how did it get chosen to mean the *Torah* if the *Torah* is supposed to be such a good thing?

The word that the scholars who translated the *Septuagint* chose to translate *Torah* was *nomos*, which means 'law' in Greek. However, at the time it conveyed the meaning 'the standard of conduct' and the sense of 'normal.' With the Gentile influx into the Church came a disconnection from the 'normal' aspect of *Torah* and it was then seen as 'the law'—a cage of outdated culturally-centered restrictions.

If we examine the laws of Canada or the United States, we discover that originally they were founded on *the* Law—*Torah*. A U.S. judge was once quoted as saying, "We have a billion laws on

---

[26] Mal. 2:3-8

the books to interpret the Ten Commandments." Another discovery we will make is that for two nations considered to be leaders of the 'free world,' we have a lot of laws! Law is preserved and enforced to insure peace and order within society. When a certain segment within society decides to live outside the common law it is called anarchy, not freedom. The biblical term for living outside of the *Torah* is not freedom either; it is 'lawlessness.'

We can see the stabilizing effect of laws even within nature: the law of gravity, the laws of motion, the laws of physics and the law of sowing and reaping, just to name a few. So we see that laws, whether of nature, of society or of God, are supposed to be a fence of protection, not a cage of restriction.

To say that the law of God is bondage is to call God an evil dictator who wanted to keep His people oppressed and 'in line.' A cursory reading of the *Tanakh* will reveal that the times when Israel was oppressed and fearful were when they were living contrary to the *Torah*. Israel's time of greatest glory were the times of David and Solomon—kings who walked in the ways of *Torah*. (Solomon at least started out that way.) To get an idea of how David felt about the law of God, read Psalm 119. In it you will find such statements as:

- *The law of Your mouth is better to me than thousands of coins of gold and silver.* (v.72)
- *Let Your tender mercies come to me, that I may live; for Your law is my delight.* (v.77)
- *Unless Your law had been my delight, I would have perished in my affliction.* (v.92)

- *Oh, how I love Your law! It is my meditation all the day.* (v.97)
- *I hate the double-minded, but I love Your law.* (v.113)

The whole of the 119th Psalm is about the *Torah*, and in it David came up with 176 different ways to tell God that he was so thankful that He had given His *Torah* to mankind. After reading this psalm, there is no way anyone can say that David felt like he was in bondage to some legalistic rules. He was expressing his understanding that it was just that law which gave him the joy of life.

2. The Unreachable Goal

Another misconception about the *Torah* is that it sets a standard that is out of reach for humanity; that God purposely put the bar so high that we would fail. What kind of a father would do that? Certainly not one who desired to see his children live in obedience to him.

Moses wanted to nip this attitude in the bud while they were still in the wilderness. He told the people in no uncertain terms,

> *"For this commandment that I command you today is not too mysterious for you, nor is it far off. It is not in heaven that you should say, 'Who will ascend into heaven for us and bring it to us that we may hear it and do it?' Nor is it beyond the sea that you should say, 'Who will go over the sea for us and bring it to us, that we may hear it and do it?' But the word is very near you, in your mouth and in your heart that you may do it."*[27]

The apostle Sha'ul quoted these verses in Romans chapter 10, showing us that he still considered them to be applicable after the 'New Covenant' had been enacted. Both Moses and Sha'ul are speaking words of encouragement to their audience; they are saying, *"You can do it!"*

3. Legalism

Another common response to any suggestion that the law of

---

[27] Dt. 30:11-14

God is applicable to believers today is that it is 'legalism.' This response is more reactive than it is educated, for a simple examination of the topic will serve to dispel the bias. As I pointed out in the section above on the *Torah* being the will of God, the instructions He has given us are expressly what He desires for us to follow. Any time we do what He has instructed or commanded, it is called *obedience*, not legalism. If we were to disregard the laws of our country with the same impunity we have toward the law of God by calling them 'legalistic,' we would find ourselves in serious trouble very quickly.

A proper definition of legalism would be a 'hyper-enforcement of humanly-imposed laws to the point of minute detail.' The legalism of the Scribes and Pharisees was not in their obedience to the *Torah*; it was in their attention to the myriad regulations that they had imposed upon themselves and added to the *Torah*. A modern example would be if you came to a full and complete stop in front of a stop sign at an intersection, and a police officer immediately pulled you over and gave you a ticket for not stopping exactly six feet in front of the sign. The law only requires you to come to a full stop; he had imposed the definition of the only spot where the stop could legally be made.

It is interesting to me to hear some of the explanations from Christians when I ask them about some of the practices and teachings of the Church. I ask, "Why is obeying the clearly written instructions of God considered legalism by the Church, but their man-made restrictions on alcohol, dancing, cards, movies, smoking, etc., considered as guidelines for proper living?" When I became a pastor, the denomination required me to sign a form declaring that I would not drink any alcohol in any form while in that capacity. It strikes me as absurd that any church would take a vehement stand against alcohol—which the Bible clearly allows us to consume in moderation—and yet allow its members to eat pork and shellfish—which the Bible is very clear on forbidding—in unlimited quantities, and then have the audacity to point a finger at me and say I was becoming legalistic.

In my book *Signpost to Freedom*, I explained how the apostle

Sha'ul had no word in his first-century vocabulary to convey the concept we think of as 'legalism.' The descriptive phrase he came up with is translated as 'under the law.' If you read the book of Galatians and substitute the phrase 'legalistic observance of *Torah*'[28] in place of 'under the law,' you will see a different message about the *Torah* emerging from his letter.

---

[28] This is how David Stern translates the Greek phrase *hupo nomon* [under the law] in his *Jewish New Testament*.

Chapter 7
What Is Its Purpose?

Perhaps the misunderstandings about *Torah* are rooted in a misconception of the purpose for which it was given to man in the first place. Most people question me as to whether we are trying to 'earn our salvation,' or they think we are teaching the message of 'salvation by works.' The answer to both of those questions is a definite 'NO!' The reason the answer is 'no' is because that is not the intention of God in giving His *Torah*.

Ever since Adam and Eve yielded to temptation that infamous day in the Garden, mankind has been dealing with a 'tainted blood scandal.' Through no choice of our own, we were infected with a spiritual disease—a disease that would make us susceptible to physical sickness and decay and, ultimately, death.

Like the fairy tale of Snow White who was lured into sampling the poison-laced apple, Eve was deceived into tasting a fig laced with the elixir of evil.[1] Adam and Eve became infected with what the ancient Jewish sages call 'the evil inclination.' It was as if the playing surface was tilted after that and man is inclined toward doing evil, like water on a sloped floor just wants to run toward the lowest point. Man was now subject to a force that would be constantly trying to pull him down; 'spiritual gravity' you could call it. Unless the pull is resisted, man's descent is inevitable.

The tree was called the Tree of the Knowledge of Good and Evil. The Hebrew word that is translated as 'knowledge' is *da'at*. It does not mean 'a mental awakening' or 'the acquisition of

---

[1] Jewish tradition says that the Tree of the Knowledge of Good and Evil was a fig tree–that's why Adam and Eve tried to cover themselves with fig leaves. The idea that it was an apple tree originated in Greek mythology.

information by our mind.' It means 'joining or union.' It is knowledge that is attained by the senses, like touching a puppy to discover that it is soft, or tasting a lemon to know that it is sour. *Da'at* is used in this same sense to describe the physical union between Adam and Eve:

And Adam knew his wife, and she conceived and bore Cain.[2]

Adam didn't just say to Eve, "Hey, I know you!" They *joined* together. In eating from that tree, Adam and Eve caused a nuclear fusion of good and evil into their DNA. Good was now joined to evil.

Ever since that happened, God has been in the process of separating. He calls His people to be holy, sanctified, set apart. He instructs them to separate clean from unclean, holy from common, righteousness from unrighteousness. He wants them to be intolerant of mixture in any form, whether it's what comes out of our mouth—sweet water or bitter as Ya'akov (James) puts it[3]— or even just not wearing a garment of wool and linen mixed together. He wants His people to be distinguishable from the world; He says, *"Come out from among them and be separate."*[4]

A. To expose sin

Torah is the line in the sand; when there is no line, there is no separation. As soon as the line is drawn, you know which side you are on. Sha'ul explains this function of *Torah* in Romans 3:20,

---

[2] Gen. 4:1
[3] Jas. 3:11
[4] 2 Cor. 6:17, quoting Isa. 52:11

*Therefore by the deeds of the law no flesh will be justified in His sight, **for by the law is the knowledge of sin.*** (emphasis mine)

The Greek word translated as 'knowledge' here does not have the same meaning as *da'at*—the *Torah* doesn't join you to sin. In this case, Sha'ul means the *Torah* shines the light of truth and exposes sin to be sin, i.e., on the wrong side of the line. He says something similar in Romans 7:7,

What shall we say then? Is the law sin? Certainly not! On the contrary, I would not have known sin except through the law.

In essence, he is saying that without the clear boundaries defined by the *Torah* he would be lost trying to discern good from evil.

John gives us an unmistakeable definition of sin in 1 John 3:4. He says,

*Whoever commits sin also commits lawlessness, **and sin is lawlessness.*** (emphasis mine)

Simply put, sin is anything outside the boundaries of *Torah*.

As mentioned earlier, there are many believers who think that those who follow *Torah* are trying to earn their own salvation. They think that way because they are ignorant of the purpose of the *Torah*. The *Torah* was not given to *produce* a relationship between God and us; it was given so we could *prove* a relationship exists. It was not given so we could *earn* our salvation; it was given so we could *express* it.

Looking again at the example of Israel, we see that they received the *Torah* after they were redeemed. From that time on, it acted as a guardian or an escort to bring people to Messiah[5]. If *Torah* didn't lead *you* to Messiah, how do you know you found the right Messiah? In these last days there is much interest in Christianity about the coming world leader who will be the antichrist. There is much speculation about who it could be. The tell-tale sign we can be watching for is that he will be a man of lawlessness, as Sha'ul explains:

> *Let no one deceive you by any means; for that Day will not come unless the falling away comes first, and **the man of sin** is revealed, the son of perdition, who opposes and exalts himself above all that is called God or that is worshipped, so that he sits as God in the temple of God, showing himself that he is God...And then **the lawless one** will be revealed, whom the Lord will consume with the breath of His mouth and destroy with the brightness of His coming. The coming of **the lawless one** is according to the working of Satan, with all power, signs, and lying wonders, and with all unrighteous deception among those who perish, **because they did not receive the love of the truth, that they might be saved. And for this reason God will send them strong delusion, that they should believe the lie, that they all may be condemned who did not believe the truth but had pleasure in unrighteousness.**[6]*
> (emphasis mine)

---

[5] Gal. 3:24
[6] 2 Thess. 2:3-4, 8-12

These are serious words from the apostle, showing us that our ultimate salvation rests on us knowing the truth so that we cannot be deceived. The man of lawlessness will come and fool many people with signs and wonders,[7] but the words coming out of his mouth will be a dead giveaway because he will reject the *Torah*. Note also that it is God Himself who is sending the strong delusion.

B. To give us a path to follow

There is no question that we are saved by grace through faith, as Sha'ul plainly states in Ephesians 2:8-9,

> *For by grace are you saved through faith, and that not of yourselves, it is the gift of God, not of works, lest anyone should boast.*

These are verses I memorized as a boy growing up in Sunday school. However, verse 10 sheds some interesting light on the previous verses. It says,

> *For we are His workmanship, created in Messiah Yeshua for good works, which God prepared beforehand that we should walk in them.*

There are two things I want to point out about this verse:
1. The good works are already determined for us, and
2. He says we should *walk in* them, not *do* them.

True obedience never comes before faith, nor is it an addition

---

[7] See also page 71 on how to recognize a false prophet.

to it, but it is always a result of it. 'Good works' are a previously set path for us to follow. Does that sound familiar? He gives us another hint at what the definition of 'good works' is in 2 Timothy 3:16,

> *All Scripture is given by inspiration of God, and is profitable for doctrine, for reproof, for correction, for instruction in righteousness, that the man of God may be complete, thoroughly equipped for every good work.*

What is the 'all Scripture' Sha'ul is talking about? The *Tanakh*. There was no New Testament at that time. So he tells Timothy, his disciple and leader in training, that the Old Testament has everything he will need to lead the congregation. More importantly, it can prepare God's people for doing the good works they should do by explaining just what they are.

C. To give us a 'target'

The Greek word used in the *B'rit Chadasha* (New Testament) to describe sin is *hamartia* which means 'to miss the mark.' I learned this as a young boy; what I wasn't taught is what 'the mark' is. As mentioned earlier, the Hebrew word *yara*—from which we get *torah*—means 'to throw, to shoot or teach with the intent of hitting the mark.' The reason the writers of the *B'rit Chadasha* chose *hamartia*—to miss the mark—to describe sin was because of its implied connection to *Torah*.

D. To light the way

In the sense of the *Torah* making a clear distinction between good and evil, right and wrong, it is likened in the Bible to light. If you've ever tried to walk on a path through the woods in the dark, you can appreciate how difficult it is. Even the tiniest flashlight can help a great deal. The more light you have, the easier it becomes and the less chance you have of being injured. It is the easiest when you have the sun to light the way; you still have to walk, but now you can see the path. That is the function of the *Torah*; it is a *'lamp to our feet and a light to our path'* as David said.

The passage quoted earlier from Isaiah chapter 2:

> *Many people shall come and say,*
> *"Come and let us go up to the mountain of the LORD*
> *To the house of the God of Jacob;*
> *He will teach us His ways,*
> *And we shall walk in His paths."*

is followed by an exhortation from Isaiah in verse 5,

> *"O house of Jacob, come and let us walk in the light of the LORD."*

Wasn't Torah just a 'temporary measure'?

This is a question commonly asked, again by those who are unfamiliar with the reason for *Torah*. After all, they may reason, "Who needs a flashlight after the sun (Son) has risen?" But there is also another side of the question that can be asked: has human nature changed in 6000 years? Do we still have the evil inclination? Has sin changed in 6000 years? Do we still need to be told what to avoid? *Does faith in Yeshua automatically guarantee that we will live righteously ever after?*

To that last question, Sha'ul gives us a definite answer. In Romans 3:21-22; 28; and 31, he wrote:

> *But now the righteousness of God apart from the law is revealed, being witnessed by the Law and the Prophets, even the righteousness of God through faith in Yeshua the Messiah, to all and on all who believe...Therefore we conclude that a man is justified by faith apart from the deeds of the law...Do we then make void the law through faith? Certainly not! On the contrary, we establish the law.* (emphasis mine)

The Greek word Sha'ul used which is translated as 'establish' has the meaning of 'to set it on firmer footing.' So instead of faith in Yeshua undermining the *Torah* in any way, it does the exact opposite.

The Torah is a covenant

The idea of covenant is relatively antiquated in modern society. We deal in contracts because we don't trust the other party. But a covenant is a mutual agreement based on trust. That agreement can be conditional or unconditional, whatever the agreeing parties decide upon. Whatever the terms of agreement, one characteristic that is true of all covenants is that it is designed to be forever.

The closest example we have in our time is the bond of marriage. (Did you just laugh?) At least in the beginning it was intended to be for all time, and that aspect of it is reflected in the vows when the bride and groom say, "'til death do us part" or some variation of the phrase; it is a forever thing as far as the participants are concerned. Even this pledge of unwavering commitment is often replaced in modern weddings with something like "as long as our love shall last." So, before the couple begins their new life together they have built in an escape hatch if either one of them becomes unhappy.

But God doesn't enter into covenants with escape clauses. He does make conditional covenants which He doesn't have to live up to if the people He made it with aren't keeping up their end, but that doesn't nullify the covenant; it just temporarily suspends it until they get back within the terms. And the *Torah* is just such a covenant—in fact it is a marriage covenant that He made with Israel at Mount Sinai. He set the terms in Exodus 19:5-6

> *"Now therefore **if** you will indeed obey my voice and keep My covenant, **then** you shall be a special treasure to Me above all people; for all the earth is mine. And you shall be to Me a kingdom of priests and a holy nation."* (emphasis mine)

This was like a prenuptial agreement between God and Israel, and it is stated in 'if ➜ then' terms. This was the betrothal ceremony where both parties promised their affection to the other. Did God know they were going to break their end of the deal? That's a no-brainer. But has He kept His end of the agreement? Yes.

In fact, if we look at God's track record regarding covenants, He's faultless.

- Is the covenant with Noah still being honoured? Every time we see a rainbow God reminds us that it is still in effect.

- How about His covenant with Abraham, Isaac and Jacob? That's why Israel was delivered out of Egypt at the exodus, not because they deserved it, but because He had promised their forefathers He would do it. In fact the present-day return of Jews from all over the world to *the land of Israel*—not Argentina or Australia like the League of Nations wanted—is in itself God's honouring of that ancient covenant with Abraham.
- How about His covenant with David? Didn't one of his descendants become THE King who is still reigning and will reign for all eternity?
- What about the 'New Covenant'? Surely you would say that is still in effect.

Then why do we put the Mosaic covenant in a separate class, that of 'temporary covenants'? Because we don't *want* it to be in effect. Since it is a conditional covenant, it requires something of us that we don't want to do.

When the underlying plan of all the covenants is understood, one discovers that each successive covenant builds upon the former one like the stories of a house. The covenant with Abraham did not make the one with Noah void, nor did the Mosaic covenant nullify the Abrahamic one.

Sha'ul illustrates it this way in Galatians 3:

Brethren, I speak in the manner of men: Though it is only a man's covenant, yet if it is confirmed, no one annuls or adds to it...What purpose does the law serve? It was added because of transgressions, till the Seed should come to whom the promise was made; and it was appointed through angels by the hand of a mediator...Is the law then against the promises of God? Certainly not! For if there had been a law given which could have given life, truly righteousness would have been by the law.[8]

He says that if a covenant is confirmed, it cannot be annulled or changed. The *Torah* did not abrogate the Abrahamic covenant; it was added to it. The law is not against the promises, and neither are the promises against the law. Why could the law not give life? According to Romans 8:3, it is because the law could not change people; it was as weak as our flesh nature. All the *Torah* could do was judge people for their failures. (We will cover this more when we discuss Sha'ul's teachings in greater detail.)

If it ain't broke...

David said, *"The law [Torah] of the LORD is perfect, converting the soul."*[9] The Hebrew word translated as 'converting' is *shuv*—the root word of *teshuva*, repentance. The word *shuv* has the connotation of 'restoring,' or 'bringing something back to its original state.' What was the original state of man's soul? There was no evil inclination, no appetite for sin. Good and evil were still separated. To walk the path of *Torah* is to walk the path of separation.

---

[8] Gal 3:15, 19, 21
[9] Ps. 19:7

Chapter 8
Yeshua's New Covenant

One detail often overlooked by most Christians when they are reading the New Testament is the fact that it assumes the underlying foundation of the previous covenants, particularly the *Torah*. One of the ways we are subtly made aware of this is by the frequent usage of terms such as these by the writers:

Witness	Testimony
Condemnation	Advocate
Judge	Judgment
Guilty	Justified
Justice	Offence
Penalty	

What do these terms have in common? They are all *legal* terms. It is the *Torah* of God that underlies the New Testament and is the foundation upon which the gospel is built. How could God sit on His throne and render the final judgments of men unless there were a law in place as a standard of measurement? If this is not the case, then His judgment can at best be arbitrary, and no one could be found guilty because they could just plead ignorance.

Yeshua's teachings about Torah

The typical Christian position on Yeshua's relationship to the *Torah* is one that says, "Yeshua fulfilled the law so we don't have to," or something like it. Another line of thought says that Yeshua was the goal of the *Torah*, so it ended at His death. But are these 'pat answers' actually based on any Scriptures, or are they merely assumed traditions that have been handed down for centuries? A simple examination of Yeshua's life and teachings will answer the question.

Fulfilled or abolished?

Early in Yeshua's ministry, He declared His position on the *Torah*. Whether He did it to refute some false information that had been disseminated about Him or merely to state His platform right from the start so no slander could be started, we don't know. But we do know what He said:

> *"Do not think that I came to destroy the Law or the Prophets. I did not come to destroy but to fulfil. For assuredly I say to you, till heaven and earth pass away, one jot or one tittle will by no means pass from the Law till all is fulfilled. Whoever therefore breaks one of the least of these commandments, and teaches men so, shall be called least in the kingdom of heaven; but whoever does and teaches them, he shall be called great in the kingdom of heaven."*[1]

In our modern vernacular, He might have said something like, *"Don't even **think** I came to destroy the law or the Prophets; get that thought out of your head!"* The Greek word translated as 'destroy' or 'abolish' is *kataluo* and it means 'to destroy, demolish, annul, deprive of force, abrogate, discard.' The word translated as 'fulfil' is *pleroo* and it means 'to make full, to fill to the full.' In first century Israel, these two terms were commonly used to describe a rabbi's teaching of *Torah*. If his interpretation and communication of the principles of the *Torah* were out of line, it would be said of him that he was 'abolishing' or 'destroying' the *Torah*, i.e., he was knocking it off its foundation, thereby causing it to be rendered ineffective in the lives of his followers. If he were interpreting and teaching it correctly, it would be said that he was 'fulfilling' the *Torah*, i.e., he was establishing it on its foundation because he was causing others to properly live out the *Torah* as it was intended to be lived out.

These two terms are mutually exclusive of each other; they

---

[1] Matt. 5:17-19

cannot both be true at the same time. Yet, by teaching and by example, Christianity advocates that by fulfilling the law Yeshua abolished it. There is no other conclusion that can be arrived at when the teaching is examined; if it is no longer in effect and binding on humanity, then it has been done away with. Yet Yeshua Himself emphatically stated to His hearers that He had not come to cause *Torah* to be rendered void. Within Judaism at the time, there was a common expectation that when Messiah came He would point out their errors in understanding the *Torah* as well as give them a *Torah* of His own. An example of this is found in the conversation between Yeshua and the woman at the well in John 4 when she said, *"I know that Messiah is coming. When He comes, He will tell us all things."*[2]

Yeshua then went on to say that not even the least little detail of the *Torah* would pass away before heaven and earth had passed away. He stated that the *Torah* (and by implication, the Prophets) would not pass away *"until all is fulfilled."* The Greek word translated 'fulfilled' in this instance is a different word than the previous one; this word is *ginomai* and means 'comes to pass, happens.' There are still many events foretold in Scripture that haven't come to pass yet, even some prophecies concerning the 'end times' or 'latter days' found within the *Torah*, so the qualifications for their being abrogated have not been met. Also note that Yeshua said that it was *"till heaven and earth pass away,"* not *"till I pass away,"* before *Torah* could be rendered ineffective. Why heaven and earth? Because they are the two witnesses Moses called when he reconfirmed the *Torah* to Israel just prior to his departure and their entering into the Promised Land.[3]

As followers of Yeshua, we are to make our goal to be like Him, to walk as He walked and live as He did. If He 'fulfilled' *Torah*, and in so doing cancelled it, then He left us no example to follow. He lived a life of obedience to the *Torah*; if we don't have to live that way, then we shouldn't follow Him and try to be

---

[2] John 4:25
[3] Deut. 30:15-20

139

like Him. He didn't show us how to live outside of the boundaries of *Torah*, and He didn't do it for a reason: we aren't supposed to live that way. In the footnotes of my Bible is a comment on the verses quoted above from Matthew 5. The comment says,

> In fulfilling the law, Jesus does not alter, replace, or nullify the commands; rather, He establishes their true intent and purpose in His teaching and accomplishes them in His obedient life.

It is a misconception to think that the 'true intent' of the commandments would in any way contradict the clear meaning of them. In the Sermon on the Mount, Yeshua didn't change the meaning of the commandments concerning adultery or murder; He built upon the existing base and intensified their application. Yet even His expansion on those commandments was not an uncommon thing within Judaism because it was based on a common Jewish principle. The principle states that a commandment consists of two parts: the physical act and its underlying moral or spiritual teaching—and neither is complete without the other. Just as it is not enough to perform the commanded deeds if they are denuded of intellectual and moral content, so it is not enough to philosophise on the commandment and seek moral improvement without actually performing the action. When one understands the proper meaning, one can obey God's will and therefore fulfil *Torah*. If properly understood and obeyed, the divine revelation provides a guide for successful living.

Another way of unravelling the misconception that 'since Yeshua kept the law perfectly, we don't have to' is in an analogy from a typical family. How many parents are there who require their firstborn child to 'toe the line' at home and get high grades in school, and then say to any siblings born after that they don't need to obey any rules or conditions because their older brother or sister already did all that? Wow! As the youngest of four children, I would have been ecstatic if my parents had said that to me! That is, until I found myself in the juvenile detention centre or jail because I had no regard for anyone else but myself. I am thankful that I was raised with definite boundaries, even though, according to my three older sisters, I did have it easier than they did.

As a final point from this section, I want to highlight that Yeshua said, *"...whoever does and teaches them* [the commandments], *he shall be called great in the kingdom of heaven."* While we may make it our goal to be great in the kingdom, we know that there will be none greater than the King Himself. In light of this, we can conclude that He both did them and taught them.

A rich young ruler

Two of the gospel writers record an incident when a young man approached Yeshua and asked Him flat out what He would have to do to attain eternal life. Possibly he had heard Yeshua teach the multitudes in parables, or had witnessed one of Yeshua's many encounters with the religious rulers, and hadn't quite caught on to what was being implied. Whatever the reason, this young man just wanted a simple straightforward answer, one that he wouldn't have to try to unscramble. Matthew remembered that it happened this way:

> *Now behold, one came and said to Him, "Good Teacher, what good thing shall I do that I may have eternal life?"*
> *So He said to him, "Why do you call Me good? No one is good but One, that is God. But if you want to enter into life, keep the commandments."*
> *He said to Him, "Which ones?"*
> *Yeshua said, "'You shall not murder,' 'You shall not commit adultery,' 'You shall not steal,' 'You shall not bear false witness,' 'Honour your father and your mother,' and*

'You shall love your neighbour as yourself.'"

The young man said to Him, "All these things have I kept from my youth. What do I still lack?"

Yeshua said to him, "If you want to be perfect, go sell what you have and give to the poor, and you will have treasure in heaven."

But when the young man heard that saying, he went away sorrowful, for he had great possessions.[4]

It is quite significant that Yeshua said the way to enter life (the young man had asked about 'eternal life') is to keep the commandments. When asked which ones specifically He was referring to, Yeshua began to list some of the Ten Commandments so the young man would get the picture, and then He added one from Leviticus 19:18 about loving your neighbour as yourself. Were these really all the commandments that were necessary to obey to obtain life eternal? No, because the young man said he had been doing these all along and still knew that he lacked something. Yeshua revealed the young man's heart when He told him to divest himself of his material goods and follow Him. Even though the young man had been outwardly obeying the commandments, Yeshua knew that he couldn't get past the one that says, "You shall have no other gods before Me."[5] The young man wasn't bowing down to any little statues, but he had placed his possessions higher on the priority list than God.

Luke remembered another instance when a lawyer asked Yeshua the same question to test Him. Yeshua responded,

"What is written in the law? How do you read it?"

So he answered and said, "You shall love the LORD your God with all your heart, with all your soul, with all your strength, and with all your mind, and your neighbour as yourself."

And He said to him, "You have answered rightly; do

---

[4] Matt. 19:16-22
[5] Ex. 20:3

this and you will live. "[6]

In both cases when Yeshua was asked point-blank the secret to finding eternal life, He affirmed that the answer lay in the law [*Torah*]—not just reading it and knowing it, but in doing it.

It is erroneous to think that we will only inherit eternal life after we die; we can have eternal life right now in this world. 'Life' has little to do with your physical body; it can make you live healthier and longer, but not make your body last forever. If we picture life as a highway (to borrow an analogy from Tom Cochrane), your body gets off at the exit marked with the date that God has foreordained; you continue on. What Yeshua was plainly saying to the young man in the first story is that the commandments are like the 'on ramps' to the highway of life. He said, "*If you would **enter** into life, keep the commandments.*" The key to us continuing on after our body has 'exited' is that we must be on the highway at the time.

Staying on the highway

So then, what is the key to staying on this 'highway of life?' We can find it in Yeshua's time of testing in the wilderness immediately after His baptism. Actually, this encounter between Yeshua and Satan is His 'clinic' on spiritual warfare. In the account told by Matthew, Satan tried to get to Yeshua through physical hunger after forty days of fasting by saying, "*If you are the Son of God, command that these stones become bread.*" I don't think that Yeshua's first thought was "Now why didn't I think of that?" like mine probably would have been. In the heat of the battle He quoted Scripture—not just any Scripture; He quoted the *Torah*.[7] He said,

*"Man shall not live by bread alone, but by **some** of the*

---

[6] Luke 10:26-28

[7] It has become very popular to quote the Scriptures when we need spiritual help, or even to pray the Scriptures during times of devotion. Whatever the reason we do it, it will be ineffective unless we are living it out in our life.

words that proceed out of the mouth of God."

No, that's not what He said. He said "...*most of the words...*"
No, that's not it either. Nor did He say, "...*all of the words that
proceed out of the mouth of God from now on.*" He said that man
lives by **every** word that proceeds from the mouth of God.[8]
Period. He was quoting Deuteronomy 8:3, where Moses is
specifically speaking about the *Torah*, the words which God
spoke directly. The *Torah* contains the only words that fall into
the category of having been spoken by the mouth of God. God
said that He would speak to other prophets through dreams and
visions, but that He spoke with Moses face to face.[9]

The Ten Commandments are known in Judaism as the 'Ten
Living Words,' not only because they are the foundational
instructions from God for living, but also because they—the
words themselves—are considered to be alive. These are what
Stephen was referencing in his defence before the Sanhedrin in
Acts 7:38. Speaking of Moses, he said, "...*the one who received
the **living oracles** [sayings] to give to us...*" This view is also
reflected in the book of Hebrews where the writer affirmed that
"***The word of God is living** and powerful, sharper than any two-
edged sword...*"

Patterning our lifestyle after any worldview or philosophy that
is not in line with what God has said is not living, i.e., walking in
life; we are only living as we 'eat' His word and then do what it
says.

Yeshua's view of 'the Word of God'

As we read the New Testament record of Yeshua's life, we
could get the impression that He was against the *Torah*, based on
all the clashes He had with the religious leaders over the
commandments. However, if we take a closer look at the issues at
the root of those verbal skirmishes, we find that the points of

---

[8] Matt. 4:4
[9] Num. 12:6-8

disagreement were not on the *validity* of the *Torah* and man's need to be subject to it; they were over the *traditions* that the Pharisees had added to *Torah* and were teaching as though they had equal weight to the written *Torah*.

A classic example of one of these confrontations is found in Mark 7:1-13. Here the Pharisees are accusing Yeshua and His disciples of breaking the commandments because they saw the disciples eating bread without washing their hands first.

> *Then the Pharisees and scribes asked Him, "Why do your disciples not walk according to the tradition of the elders, but eat bread with unwashed hands?"*
>
> *He answered and said to them, "Well did Isaiah prophesy of you hypocrites, as it is written:*

> 'This people honours Me with their lips,
> But their heart is far from Me.
> And in vain do they worship Me,
> Teaching as doctrines the commandments of men.'

> ***For laying aside the commandment of God, you hold to the tradition of men**—the washing of pitchers and cups, and many other such things you do."*
>
> *He said to them, "All too well you reject the commandment of God, that you may keep your tradition. For Moses said, 'Honour your father and your mother;' and 'He who curses father or mother, let him be put to death.' But you say, 'If a man says to his father or mother, "Whatever profit you might have received from me is Corban"—(that is, a gift to God)', then you no longer let him do anything for his father or mother, **making the word of God of no effect through your tradition** which you have handed down. And many such things you do."*[10]

In this encounter, Yeshua not only makes a clear distinction

---

[10] Mark 7:5-13

between the commandments of God and the Pharisees' 'precious' traditions, but in the process He plainly equates the commandments of God with the word of God, just as we saw that the Prophets had done before Him.

What is the 'Great Commission'?

The selection of verses we looked at earlier in Matthew 5 also had something to say about what Yeshua taught, and in turn, what He expects His followers to teach. The verses said,

> *"Whoever therefore breaks one of the least of these commandments, **and teaches men so,** shall be called least in the kingdom of heaven; but whoever does **and teaches them,** he shall be called great in the kingdom of heaven."*

Of course it is without question that Yeshua is the greatest in the kingdom of heaven—He is the King. So we can naturally deduce that He not only *did* the commandments, but *taught* them as well. But what about His commission to His followers—what should we be teaching?

The section known as 'the Great Commission' is found in Matthew 28:19-20:

> *"Go therefore and make disciples of all the nations, baptizing them in the name of the Father and of the Son and of the Holy Spirit, **teaching them to observe all things that I have commanded you;** and lo, I am with you always, even to the end of the age."* (emphasis mine)

What had He commanded them to do? This is a crucial question, because it will determine what we are to be teaching all the nations.

Two key words in this commission will unlock the mystery of what He commanded us. The first is 'observe;' it is an action word. He didn't say, "...*teaching them to **believe** everything I* *said.*" He indicated that there is to be a resulting action accompanying the teaching. The second word is 'commanded;' the parallel is obvious. In all His time of ministry, Yeshua only gave one new commandment, that we love one another as He loves us.[11] So what were (are) these commandments?

The night before He was crucified, He said, *"If you love Me, keep My commandments."*

As the Word made flesh, would His commandments be any different than the ones in the *Torah*—the written Word? He Himself said, *"I only say what My Father tells Me to say."*[12] Had the Father changed His mind? No; therefore Yeshua's commandments are identical to God's commandments. I recently heard Messianic leader Daniel Juster speak at a conference, and he made the statement that, "The Church is not preaching the gospel of the kingdom until it is teaching people to obey everything that Yeshua commanded us to do." Unless someone tells them the truth, they are in for a rude awakening.

Scary verses in the Bible

At the end of the Sermon on the Mount, the one Yeshua began with the statement, *"Don't think I came to abolish the Law and the Prophets…"* He concludes with a hypothetical scenario of Judgment Day. (In actuality, it wasn't really hypothetical because He said that it will happen.) He described the scene like this:

> *"Not everyone who says to Me, 'Lord, Lord,' shall enter the kingdom of heaven, but **he who does the will of My Father** in heaven. Many will say to Me in that day, 'Lord, Lord, have we not prophesied in Your name, cast out demons in Your name, and done many wonders in Your name?' And then I will declare to them, 'I never knew you; depart from Me, **you who practice lawlessness**.'"*[13]

---

[11] John 13:34
[12] John 12:49-50
[13] Matt. 7:21-23

(emphasis mine)

The first thing we notice is that it is not what we *say* that will gain us entrance to the kingdom, but what we *do*—the will of God. As pointed out earlier, 'the will of God' was understood in Jewish culture to mean obeying the commandments. Actually, this section is an expanded doublet, a Hebrew manner of repeating something in a different way for emphasis and clarification. In the first sentence, He says that he who does the Father's will *will* enter the kingdom, and in the second He says that those who 'practice lawlessness' *will not* get in.

These people are believers—charismatic, Bible-totin', devil-destroyin', miracle-workin' believers...or so they think. You can't say they are doing these things out of false motives; they are sincere. You can't say they don't think they are following Yeshua, they call Him 'Lord.' So why will they be rejected? They will be rejected on the basis of how they lived, not the signs and wonders they did. Yeshua described them as 'lawless' (Gk. *anomia*: opposed to the law)—i.e., not living according to the commandments in the *Torah*. His final statement to them will be "*I never knew you.*"

These are sobering words from Yeshua, and they should make each and every one who claims to be a believer reconsider his or her relationship with Him. Do we know Him? How do we know if we know Him? We can't just say, "I know that I know that I know," because that is just 'Christianese' for "I don't know." The Bible gives us a clear criterion for determining whether we actually know Him or not. It can be found in 1 John 2.

> *My little children, these things I write to you that you may not sin. And if anyone sins, we have an Advocate with the Father, Yeshua HaMashiach the righteous. And He Himself is the propitiation for our sins, and not for ours only but also for the whole world. **Now by this we know that we know Him, if we keep His commandments. He who says, "I know Him" and does not keep His***

commandments, is a liar, and the truth is not in him. But whoever keeps His word, truly the love of God is perfected in him. By this we know that we are in Him. He who says he abides in Him ought himself also to walk just as He walked.[14] (emphasis mine)

I don't think John could have put it any clearer. When I make statements like these, people get downright upset, so I just show them where it is in the Bible. It can't be interpreted any other way: we can only say we know Him if we are keeping His commandments. A major part of the reason why the Church is not following the commandments stems from the fact that they have been introduced to a counterfeit Messiah, one who does not require anything of them, has no definite commandments, whose 'grace and mercy' is basically license to live as they want, and who will never leave them or forsake them no matter what. That is not the Messiah of the Bible.

Yeshua didn't fulfil the *Torah* so we don't have to; He did it so we, too, could do it correctly. The only thing He did so that we don't have to is pay for our sin, because we couldn't do it. He didn't *live* for us; He *died* for us so that *we* could live for *Him*.

The New Covenant

Matt 26:28.

At His death, Yeshua confirmed a 'new' covenant.[15] What is this new covenant? When He spoke those words that night in the upper room while celebrating Passover with His disciples, why didn't He explain what this 'new covenant' was all about? The reason is because the disciples knew exactly what He meant. They may not have picked up on all the details for another three days, but they knew what He was referring to. There is only one place in the Old Testament where the phrase 'new covenant' is used, and it is found in Jeremiah 31:

---

[14] 1 John 2:1-6
[15] Matt. 26:28

*"Behold, the days are coming, says the LORD, when I will make **a new covenant** with the house of Israel and the house of Judah—not according to the covenant that I made with their fathers in the day that I took them by the hand to lead them out of Egypt, My covenant which they broke, though I was a husband to them, says the LORD. **But this is the covenant that I will make with the house of Israel after those days, says the LORD: I will put My law in their minds, and write it on their hearts;** and I will be their God, and they shall be My people. No more shall every man teach his neighbour, and every man his brother, saying, 'Know the LORD,' for **they shall all know Me**, from the least of them to the greatest of them, says the LORD. For I will forgive their iniquity, and their sin I will remember no more."*

The content of the covenant is *Torah*, only this time the LORD isn't going to write it on tablets of stone but on fleshy tablets of the heart. The result will be that all of His people shall 'know Him,' from the least to the greatest.

When Christians tell me that they are 'new covenant believers,' I ask them whether they are part of Israel or Judah, since those are the only two groups with whom the 'new covenant' ('new testament' in Latin) is made. I also ask them if they are walking in the covenant or breaking it like the people in the wilderness did.

That this is the 'new covenant' that the early believers understood Yeshua to have initiated is clear from the book of Hebrews. The writer quotes these verses from Jeremiah in Hebrews 8:8-12 with the following commentary, starting with verse 6:

[6] *But now He has obtained a more excellent ministry, inasmuch as He is also Mediator of a better covenant, which was established on better promises.* [7] *For if that first had been faultless, then no place would have been sought for a second.* [8] *Because finding fault with them, He says,*

"Behold, the days are coming...

[13] *In that He says, "A new covenant," He has made the first obsolete. Now what is becoming obsolete and growing old is ready to vanish away."*

In all of chapter seven and eight of Hebrews, the writer is comparing the High Priest, from the order of Aaron, to Yeshua, who is from the order of Melchizedek. Yeshua is the Mediator of the *'better* [new] *covenant, which was established on better promises.'* However, there is something hidden from our view by the translators in verse 6: the phrase 'which was established' is the same in the Greek as the words *'received the law'* in 7:11. In *The Compete Jewish Bible*, David H. Stern correctly translates verse 6:

> *"For this covenant has been given as Torah on the basis of better promises."*

In his *Jewish New Testament Commentary*, he says this about the blatant omission from most versions:

> This is a virtually unknown theological truth of far-reaching importance. First, although there are many, both Jews and Christians, who suppose that the New Testament abrogated the *Torah*, the New Testament here explicitly states that it has itself been given as *Torah*. Obviously, if the New Testament is *Torah*, then the *Torah* has not been abrogated. Instead, the New Testament has been given the same status as the *Torah* of Moses; that is, it has come to have the highest authority there is, the authority that accompanies promulgation by God Himself. One might say that *Torah* has been expanded – or, better, that *Torah* has been made more explicit.
>
> And it means that a Gentile grafted into Israel by his faith in Yeshua the Messiah has himself come into the framework of Israel's *Torah*…
>
> That the New Covenant has become *Torah* is absolutely crucial for understanding the New Testament.

Yet so far as I know, not one existing translation brings out this truth; nor, to my knowledge, does any commentary so much as mention it.[16]

The writer of Hebrews goes on to say in verse 7, "*For if that first had been faultless, then no place would have been sought for a second,*" seemingly implying that the *Torah* was a faulty covenant. However, the writer makes very plain in verse 8 where the fault was: "*... finding fault with **them**.*" The *Torah* was in no way to blame for the peoples' disobedience; it was their unwillingness to resist the evil inclination within their own hearts.

The part in verse 13 which says that "*He has made the first obsolete*" again seems to imply that it is the *Torah* which is being 'mothballed.' But when we take this comment in the context of the verses he quoted from Jeremiah, we realize that it would be totally incongruous to make that conclusion. Why would he go to the trouble to establish the content of the 'new covenant' as the *Torah* being written on our hearts and then immediately say that the *Torah* is defunct? What is being made obsolete is the *Torah* as *an external body of guidelines and instructions* because in the new covenant He is endeavouring to make them an *internal conviction* within us.

The *Torah*, as it was given at Mt. Sinai, can be likened to one of those white signs beside the road with the big black numbers. Although it can clearly tell us what the government has determined to be the maximum safe speed at which to travel, it is powerless to actually make us stay below that limit. If I want to travel at a higher speed, I can; but if I choose to do so, I am a lawbreaker and can suffer the consequences. That sign is really only as effective as my human nature wants it to be. The power of the sign is weakened by my 'flesh.' However, if I want to be a law-abiding citizen, I will internalise that speed limit and keep my speed in check. I am not doing it out of fear of the consequences; I am doing it out of respect for those who made the law, believing that they know more than I do about driving safety. If I think that

---

[16] *Jewish New Testament Commentary*, p. 687-688

limit was put there purposely to annoy me or for people who don't really know how to drive, then I will probably disregard it. If I think it was set for my protection and the protection of the other drivers and their families, then I will most likely obey it.

The agent whereby the *Torah* is written on our hearts and in our minds is none other than the Holy Spirit. In a prophecy given to Ezekiel about this same time of the 'new covenant,' the LORD spoke this:

> *"I will give you a new heart and put a new spirit within you; I will take the heart of stone out of your flesh and give you a heart of flesh. I will put My Spirit within you and cause you to walk in My statutes and you will keep My judgments and do them."*[17]

This is probably where Sha'ul got the idea for the illustration:

> *"Clearly you are an epistle of Messiah, ministered by us, written not with ink but by the Spirit of the living God, not on tablets of stone, but on tablets of flesh, that is, of the heart."*[18]

The prophecy of Ezekiel clearly shows that the purpose behind God pouring out His Holy Spirit into the hearts of people is to influence us to desire to be obedient to His instructions—His statutes and judgments. That's why it was poured out on the Day of Pentecost, or *Shavu'ot*, because it was the same day—the same 'appointed time'—as when He gave the *Torah* to Moses on the mountain. The first time He wrote them on stone; the second time He wrote them on flesh. When He writes on us—when we *let* Him write on us—we become His epistle, known and read by all men.

In Hebrews 9:15 the writer states, *"He is the mediator of the new covenant, by means of death..."* In verse 18, he confirms that

---

[17] Ezk. 36:26-27
[18] 2 Cor. 3:3

"not even the first covenant was confirmed without blood." He again quotes those same verses from Jeremiah 31 in chapter 10:16-17 to make sure his readers (us) get the definition of the 'new covenant' that Yeshua ratified with His blood. Then he goes on to write some ominous words:

> *For if we sin willfully after we have received the knowledge of the truth, there no longer remains a sacrifice for sins, but a certain fearful expectation of judgment, and fiery indignation, which will devour the adversaries. Anyone who has rejected Moses' law dies without mercy on the testimony of two or three witnesses. Of how much worse punishment, do you suppose, will he be thought worthy who has trampled the Son of God underfoot, counted the blood of the covenant by which he was sanctified a common thing, and insulted the Spirit of grace? For we know Him who said, 'Vengeance is Mine, I will repay' says the LORD. And again, 'The LORD will judge His people.'*[19]

Why is it that Christians don't think these verses apply to them? He says, *"If WE sin willfully..."* and *"The LORD will judge HIS people."* But notice some other important points he makes:

- That *he who has rejected Moses' law **dies*** (present tense in the Greek) *without mercy.* No qualifications, no exemptions, no disclaimers. This was written *after* the 'new covenant' was in effect.
- That 'dying without mercy' will seem trite compared to the retribution the LORD will measure out on those who reject the blood of the 'new covenant' and treat it as a common thing. Who are these people? Anyone who continues to live as though Yeshua's blood was not effective in confirming the new covenant, i.e., the Law of God, the *Torah*, being written in their heart.
- That the Spirit of grace (the Holy Spirit) is insulted when

---

[19] Heb. 10:26-31

the new covenant is rejected. Why? Because we refuse to let Him write the *Torah* on our heart.

This new covenant that Yeshua confirmed by shedding His blood is not the simple "now-everyone-gets-a-free-ticket-into-heaven-if-you-only-raise-your-hand-and-repeat-the-sinners'-prayer-after-me" message hawked by Christianity to get people in the door and then keep them there. It is a serious life-encompassing commitment to learn the way of the LORD and then walk in it.

Chapter 9
What Yeshua's Followers Taught

While Yeshua was on earth, He gathered twelve men around Him to be His disciples. These men were the ones in whom He invested most of His ministry and with whom He spent a majority of His time. The miracles and public teaching were really a secondary purpose for His coming; even the message of His substitutionary death might have been lost in the scrapbooks of history had He not trained others to carry the gospel of the kingdom after His departure. It is from the teachings and writings of these men that we can gain a window into the tutelage they received from the Messiah, how they understood His position on the *Torah* and how they, in turn, taught the early believers. If His life and death abrogated the message of the *Torah*, then we should see that theme echoed strongly and consistently throughout their writings; if He endorsed and modelled a *Torah* lifestyle, then we should see that reflected in His followers' lives.

Let's begin our search for evidence with two of the men considered to be the 'leaders' of His disciples and the early believers: James and John.

John

Earlier in this section, it was from John's writings that we derived the definition of sin, that *sin is lawlessness*. We also looked previously at a passage from 1 John 2 where John said,

> "*Now by this we know that we know Him, if we keep His commandments. He who says, 'I know Him,' and does not keep His commandments, is a liar, and the truth is not in him.*"

Now I suppose some could say that the 'His' can be ambiguous as to whose commandments we are to keep, but these next verses will clear up any confusion.

*If someone says, "I love God," and hates his brother, he is a liar; for he who does not love his brother whom he has seen, how can he love God whom he has not seen? And this commandment we have from Him: that he who loves God must love his brother also...By this we know that we love the children of God, **when we love God and keep His commandments. For this is the love of God, that we keep His commandments.** And His commandments are not burdensome.* [1] (emphasis mine)

Here John is showing the organic connection between the commandments to 'Love the LORD your God with all your heart, etc.,' and 'Love your neighbour as yourself." The two cannot be separated in any way, and, in fact, John shows that loving our brother is wrapped up in loving God. Then he delivers the unquestionable definition of what loving God is: keeping His [God's] commandments.

Loving God has been soft-pedalled for centuries as a feeling we have, an emotional high, an indefinable experience—yet the definition has been right here all along. Yeshua said the same thing: *"If you love Me, keep My commandments."* Saying we love Him without showing we love Him puts us in the same category as the people Isaiah prophesied against when the LORD said through Him:

"...these people draw near with their mouths and honour Me with their lips, but have removed their hearts far from Me." [2]

In any lasting relationship, the parties know what the other does and does not like. In our marriage, for instance, my wife knows what pleases me and what annoys me. There are some items that we disagree on, that she likes and I don't, or vice versa. It is in the recognition of those differences that we can say "I love

---

[1] 1 John 4:20-21; 5:2-3
[2] Isa. 29:13

you" by our actions. For example, if she were to constantly serve me pickled beets (one of her favourites, but not on my 'Top 1000' list) she would not be showing love to me. If I hadn't told her I don't care for them, or if I hadn't told her what I like to eat, then it would be different. It is the same in our relationship with God: He has told us what He wants us to do, i.e., how we can show our love to Him. If we continue to do the things *we* enjoy doing (and getting the emotional high from), we are not loving Him but disregarding Him altogether.

The last line from the verses quoted from 1 John 5 says, *"And His commandments are not burdensome."* A while ago, Pamela discovered something about this verse rather serendipitously. She was looking up the word *torah* in a Hebrew Lexicon, but was looking it up as if it began with the letter 'tet' rather than a 'tav' since both have the 't' sound in Hebrew. What she found was the Hebrew word *torach*, which means 'burden.' What John was thinking in Hebrew when (if) he was writing in Greek was *'Torah* is not *torach'*: the *Torah* is not a burden.

Ya'akov (James)[3]

There is extra-biblical evidence that gives us some insight into who this man was and how he lived. The ancient historians Hegesippus, Josephus, and Eusebius all make mention of him in their writings. In the introduction in my Bible to the book of James, the editors included this information:

> The early church historian Hegesippus identified him as 'James the Just,' testifying to his extraordinary godliness, his zeal for obedience to the law of God, and his singular devotion to prayer.

In light of this evidence, I ask, "What kind of a book would a man like this write?" Certainly not one that would speak

---

[3] The Ya'akov who wrote the book was not the brother of John; he was the brother of Yeshua and the leader of the Jerusalem congregation soon after Yeshua's resurrection.

derogatorily of the *Torah*, nor one that would diminish its importance to a believer. Martin Luther called this letter 'the epistle of straw'—i.e., of no value—because of Ya'akov's statement, *"Faith without works is dead."* Luther had recently come into the awareness of justification by faith[4] and, at least in Luther's mind, Ya'akov contradicted that position. Ya'akov understood the importance of backing up our words with actions. Luther did the Church a disservice by fostering the misconception that faith alone is enough, whereas Ya'akov said, *"even the demons believe and tremble."* Ya'akov even asked the rhetorical question (probably sarcastically):

What does it profit, my brethren, if someone says he has faith but does not have works? ***Can faith save him?***[5]

He closes this section by saying,

You see then that a man is justified [made righteous] *by works, and not by faith.*[6]

Earlier in his letter he wrote,

*But be doers of the word, and not hearers only, deceiving yourselves. For if anyone is a hearer of the word and not a doer, he is like a man observing his natural face in a mirror; for he observes himself, goes away, and immediately forgets what kind of man he was. But he who looks into **the perfect law of liberty** and continues in it, and is not a forgetful hearer but a doer of **the work**, this one will be blessed in what he does.*[7]

In this section he equates 'the word' with a mirror—something that shows us what we are like—only this mirror

---

[4] Rom. 5:1
[5] Jas. 2:14
[6] Jas. 2:24
[7] Jas. 1:22-25

reveals what is inside us. He then discloses that this word/mirror is the 'perfect law of liberty,' i.e., the *Torah*. There is only one law which is described as being perfect, and that is the *Torah* as described by David in Psalm 19:7. Ya'akov explains that this word/mirror shows us how God intends us to be, and that when, by our choices, we don't look like 'the man in the mirror,' it is because we have forgotten what manner of people we were. When we read His *Torah*, we see that He has set His people apart as holy and righteous and has shown them how to live holy and righteously. The description in the *Torah* is who He made us when He made us righteous.

He says that if we are only listening to the words but not doing the work [of keeping the commandments], we are self-deceived into thinking that we can receive a blessing. It is the one who is aligning his actions with the words of *Torah* who will be blessed.

The issue of Torah for the Gentiles

This 'James' is the one who was the leader of the congregation in Jerusalem, and was presiding at the council meeting recounted in Acts 15. The issue on the table was the applicability of the *Torah* to Gentiles...or so we have been led to believe. The real issue is stated in verse 1:

> And certain men came down from Judea and taught the brethren, "Unless you are circumcised according to the custom of Moses, you cannot be saved."

These Jewish men had taken the stance that no Gentile could be saved without first becoming a Jew. Circumcision was the last rite of conversion to Judaism, and these guys said that without doing that, there was no salvation.[8] So the thorny issue the

---

[8] This happened while Sha'ul was in Galatia, and it prompted him to make the trip to Jerusalem and get the problem ironed out, then to write the book of Galatians to settle the issue in the minds of the people living there. I have covered this in greater detail in my book *Signpost to Freedom*, so I will not go into it here.

council is debating in Acts 15 is 'do Gentiles need to convert to Judaism (become Jews) in order to be saved?' In the midst of their discussion, the topic comes up as to whether they (the Gentiles) should be expected to keep the *Torah*. There are three key points to notice about this deliberation, which reveal their conclusion on the matter:

1. That Gentiles (non-Jews) could be included in the group called 'the people of God' was established in the Tanakh. This is evidenced by Ya'akov quoting from Amos 9:11-12 about the LORD rebuilding the tabernacle of David *"So that the rest of mankind may seek the LORD, even all the Gentiles who are called by My name."*

   Isaiah also spoke about this in 56:3-5 where he says the sons of the foreigner who keep His Sabbath and His covenant will be given a place in His house better than that of sons and daughters.

2. The list of regulations the council decides upon for the Gentiles to observe is a very short list. It doesn't even cover all of the Ten Commandments! If this were truly all the Gentiles had to do, then it would be a cakewalk. There are no prohibitions against stealing, murdering, coveting, breaking the Sabbath or taking the name of the LORD in vain. Can this be right? No.

   The list given by the apostles of the council contained the actions that the Gentiles must stop in order to gain acceptance within the (at that time) overwhelmingly Jewish group of believers. It also was not their attempt to update the Noahide laws, which Jews see as incumbent upon all men. How can we be so sure of this conclusion?

3. In verse 21 Ya'akov says, *"For Moses has had throughout many generations those who preach him in every city, being read in the synagogues every Sabbath."* The understood implication is that they

[the Gentiles] will get the rest of the necessary instruction by going to the synagogue each Sabbath.

This issue of whether or not the Gentiles were required to follow the *Torah* hasn't been raised for centuries. The Jews resolved the matter in their minds by posing one of two solutions: first, that non-Jews were only required to adhere to the Noahide laws, those that were set in place by God after the flood, deduced from Genesis, chapter nine[9]; and second, that if a non-Jew wanted to follow the instructions of God, he or she must undergo conversion and become a Jew. Either way, the Jews' answer to the question whether Gentiles must observe *Torah* was 'No.'

The Gentile response to the question was also a definite 'no' after they broke away from Judaism and all things Jewish. In order to give the *Torah* some measure of respect, they categorized the laws into three parts: moral, ceremonial and judicial. Those laws that were judged to still be of moral or judicial benefit were retained; the others were discarded. It is worth noting that nowhere in Scripture do we find God ever making any distinctions like these; to Him they are all equally valid.

As I stated earlier, it was a question on this very issue that began my quest that brought me to the point where I am today. The question was, "Why would God set aside the Jews because of unfaithfulness to His covenant, but then turn to the Gentiles and say that they didn't have to keep the covenant at all? Wouldn't it have been more appropriate for Him to just say to the Jews, 'I tell you what; let's just chalk this whole *Torah* thing up to a bad idea and start all over from scratch. I'll send My Son and He will give you the new guidelines.' " Did God change? Did He change His

---

[9] The Noahide laws are:
    1. the establishment of law courts
   Prohibition against:
    2. blasphemy
    3. sexual immorality
    4. idolatry
    5. murder
    6. theft
    7. eating a limb torn from a living animal (compassion for animals)

mind? Are there two standards of righteousness, one for Jew and another for Gentile?

As I pointed out earlier in the book, the 'new covenant' was only to be made with the house of Judah and the house of Israel. The only way a Gentile can be included in this covenant is by being adopted into the family. Israel (the Jewish people) is the firstborn son.[10] An adopted child has no different rules than a natural born one, and therefore would be expected to uphold the same standards of behaviour.

Sha'ul (Paul), Apostle to the Gentiles

Typically, when I discuss the validity of the *Torah* with a Christian, their objections are rooted in the writings of the apostle Sha'ul. I understand that Sha'ul was a brilliant man, extremely well educated; he said that he 'advanced in Judaism beyond many of my contemporaries in my own nation.' I acknowledge that he was a powerful speaker (probably a lawyer); he was zealous for his cause; he was without doubt an anointed apostle. But he was not the Messiah; therefore, we must judge his words by the words of Yeshua.

A common response when I question people about the system of their beliefs is, "You go however you want; I'll stick with Paul!" That response begs the question, "Do you know what Paul taught?" The standard Christian's conception of Sha'ul is that of a man who was raised in Judaism and then, after his encounter with Yeshua, did an 'about face' and promptly discarded as garbage everything he'd ever been taught. In fact, it is often said that Sha'ul was the originator of Christianity rather than Yeshua. But let's take a look at what he had to say.

Reading through the book of Acts with an open mind will let us see a Sha'ul who is much different than the one commonly known. In there, as well as in his writings, we discover a man who never lost his zeal for the *Torah*. In his defence before the Jewish Sanhedrin, he claimed that he was a Pharisee, to which the

---

[10] Ex. 4:22

other Pharisees in the crowd responded, "We find no evil in this man."[11] In his defence in front of the Roman governor Felix, he stated that he still believed *everything* that was written in the Law and the Prophets. Later, when Festus replaced Felix as governor, Sha'ul told him "Neither against the law of the Jews, nor against the temple, nor against Caesar have I offended in anything at all."

In Acts 21 is an account of when Sha'ul returned to Jerusalem from one of his ministry trips. He was confronted by the apostles who told him there was a rumour going around that he was teaching all the Jews who live among the Gentiles to forsake Moses, i.e., the *Torah*, not to circumcise their children, and to disregard the [Jewish] customs. Then they gave him a chance to clear his reputation and quell the rumour so that everyone would know that *"you yourself also walk orderly and keep the law."* At this watershed moment, a time when Sha'ul could have made his definitive statement against the *Torah* and Judaism, he followed through with disproving the false report.[12] He proved that he never taught anyone to abandon the *Torah*.

His writings

The book of Romans is thought to be the pinnacle of Christian doctrine, the summit of Pauline systematic theology. It was written near the end of the apostle's life and therefore should contain the clearest and purest instruction on living the life that God expects of a believer. This book has been a well of inspiration for thousands of preachers over the centuries because of that very fact. Martin Luther was awakened from the deadness of the Roman Catholic Church by Sha'ul's proclamation in 5:1 that we have been 'justified by faith.' Countless theologians have written countless volumes on this short book. (It actually is a letter, and as *letters* go, it is quite long, but as *books* go, it is quite short.) However, to go about correctly interpreting the message of this epistle, we must remember the mindset of its writer and his

---

[11] Ac. 23:9

[12] Many Church historians place this incident *after* Sha'ul wrote the book of Galatians.

position on the *Torah*.

We can begin by looking at the topic of justification by faith that signalled the end of the dark ages and the dawn of a new era. When I was a boy growing up in Sunday school, I was taught that 'justification' meant 'just-as-if-I'd-never-sinned,' which is actually a pretty fair summation of the concept. As mentioned earlier, it is a legal term that carries the meaning of a state of innocence or of 'having your slate wiped clean.' Sha'ul begins laying the foundation of this vital truth in chapter 3:

> *Now we know that whatever the law says, it says to those who are under the law, that every mouth may be stopped, and all the world may become guilty before God.* ***Therefore by the deeds of the law no flesh will be justified in His sight,*** *for by the law is the knowledge of sin.*
>
> *But now the righteousness of God apart from the law is revealed, being witnessed by the Law and the Prophets, even the righteousness of God, through faith in Yeshua the Messiah, to all and on all who believe. For there is no difference; for all have sinned and fall short of the glory of God, being justified freely by His grace through the redemption that is in Messiah Yeshua, whom God set forth as a propitiation by His blood, through faith, to demonstrate His righteousness, because in His forebearance God has passed over the sins that were previously committed, to demonstrate at the present time His righteousness, that He might be just and the justifier of the one who has faith in Yeshua.*[13] (emphasis mine)

What is hidden from view in this English rendition of this section is the fact that the words 'justification' and 'righteousness' are from the same word in the Greek text, showing us that to be justified is to be made righteous. What Sha'ul wants to make very clear to his readers is that no one is justified/made righteous by observing the law; that's not why it was given. Our slate is

---

[13] Rom. 3:19-26

cleared by faith in the blood of Yeshua (notice the subliminal 'pass over' reference in verse 25). He is not teaching them to disregard *Torah;* he's teaching them not to misuse it. No amount of *Torah* observance can bring a person to justification; if it could, then faith would be unnecessary.

How can I be so sure this is his point? If we continue reading verses 27-31, he finishes the thought:

> *Where is boasting then? It is excluded. By what law? Of works? No, but by the law of faith. Therefore we conclude that a man is justified by faith apart from the deeds of the law. Or is He the God of the Jews only? Is He not also the God of the Gentiles? Yes, of the Gentiles also, since there is one God and He will justify the circumcised by faith and the uncircumcised through faith.* **Do we then make void the law through faith? Certainly not! On the contrary, we establish the law.** (emphasis mine)

His message is that believing in Yeshua doesn't *cancel* the *Torah*; it *confirms* it. What is the 'faith' he is speaking of? Is it just simply 'believing' with our mind? No; having faith *in* Yeshua means that we are faithful *to* Him by following His example. He lived a life that gave con*firm*ation to the *Torah* by con*form*ation to it.

Moving ahead to chapter 5 of Romans, we find another loaded sentence:

> *Therefore, just as through one man sin entered the world, and death through sin, and thus death spread to all men, because all sinned—for until the law, sin was in the world but sin is not imputed when there is no law. Nevertheless,* **death reigned from Adam to Moses,** *even over those who had not sinned according to the likeness of Adam, who is a type of Him who was to come.*[14] (emphasis mine)

---

[14] Rom. 5:12-14

Why did he say that death reigned from Adam until Moses? Surely he meant from Adam to Yeshua...or did he? What was it that happened in Moses' lifetime that had the power to stop the reign of death? The giving of the *Torah*. Walking in *Torah* by faith is the pathway of life, everlasting life.

Chapter 7 opens with another curious statement:

Or do you not know, brethren (for I speak to those who know the law) that the law has dominion over a man as long as he lives?

Notice that he identifies his readers (commonly thought to be Gentiles) as those who are more than just familiar with the law, but who *know* it. Then he goes on to matter-of-factly state what they already know, that the law is applicable to anyone who is alive. We addressed verse 7 earlier when we used it to show that the law sets the boundaries of sin:

What shall we say then? Is the law sin? Certainly not! On the contrary, I would not have known sin except through the law.

And he concludes in verses 12 and 14:

*Therefore the law is holy, and the commandment holy and just and good...For **we know that the law is spiritual** [lit. 'of the Spirit'] but I am carnal, sold under sin.* (emphasis mine)

Here he begins the carnal (fleshly)/spiritual motif that will carry on into chapter 8. Later in chapter 7, he introduces another law, that of sin and death, which is in direct contrast to the *Torah*, the law of God. This sets the groundwork for the following:

There is therefore now no condemnation to those who are

in Messiah Yeshua. *For the law of the spirit of life in Messiah Yeshua* [Torah] *has made me free from the law of sin and death. For what the law* [Torah] *could not do, in that it was weak through* [lit. 'weakened by'] *the flesh, God did by sending His own son in the likeness of sinful flesh, on account of sin* [lit. 'as a sin offering']; *He condemned sin in the flesh, that the righteous requirement of the law* [Torah] *might be fulfilled in us who do not walk according to the flesh but according to the Spirit. For those who live according to the flesh set their minds on the things of the flesh, but those who live according to the Spirit, the things of the Spirit. For to be carnally minded is death, but to be spiritually minded is life and peace. Because the carnal mind is enmity against God; for it is not subject to the law of God* [Torah]*, nor indeed can be. So then, those who are in the flesh cannot please God.* (emphasis mine)

This section is saturated with pro-*Torah* implications. Sha'ul says that *'the law of the spirit of life in Messiah Yeshua has made me free from the law of sin and death.'* The 'law of sin and death' is *not* the *Torah* as is commonly taught in Christianity; it is the law that wars *against* the *Torah* as Sha'ul revealed in chapter 7. Simply put, the law of sin and death is 'if you sin, you will die' or as he said it in 6:23, *"The wages of sin is death."*

The *Torah* was 'weak through the flesh' because it is only as strong as our flesh. Its purpose is to point the way, but it cannot make us go that way. Therefore it is in and of itself powerless. But notice that even though God sent His Son as a sin offering, there are still righteous requirements of the Law that must be fulfilled, and that can only happen as we walk in the Spirit. He tells us that those who live/walk according to the Spirit are focused on the things of the Spirit. What are the things of the Spirit? He told us back in 7:14 that *the law* is of the Spirit.

He then gives us a definitive description of what being 'carnal—or fleshly—minded' is in verse 7, that it is when someone is not subjecting himself to the Law of God—the *Torah*. He then states without qualification that someone who is not ordering his or her life according to the law of God *cannot* please Him. Although he didn't write it in this paragraph, it is implied that someone who is walking in the Spirit *is* submitted to the *Torah*, and that person *is* pleasing God by doing so.

There are many examples I could give from Sha'ul's writings which clearly show a positive attitude toward the *Torah*, but I will only include a few more. In 1 Corinthians 7:19 he wrote:

> *Circumcision is nothing, and uncircumcision is nothing,* ***but keeping the commandments of God is what matters.*** (emphasis mine)

There is no way this statement can be twisted to mean anything other than the *Torah*.

In 2 Corinthians 3:2-6, we find this allusion to *Torah* as the 'new covenant:'

> *You are our epistle written in our hearts, known and read by all men; clearly you are an epistle of Messiah, ministered by us,* ***written not with ink but by the Spirit of the living God, not on tablets of stone, but on tablets of flesh, that is, of the heart.***
> *And we have such trust through Messiah toward God...who also made us sufficient as ministers of* ***the new covenant,*** *not of the letter but of the spirit; for the letter kills, but the spirit gives life.* (emphasis mine)

The part about something being written on the heart sounds familiar, doesn't it? And the 'new covenant' that Sha'ul claims to be a minister of, what was that again? You will find when you allow the Bible to speak for itself, it becomes amazingly clear.

If Sha'ul had known that believers would so elevate his own writings that they would abandon the reading of the *Torah* in favour of reading them, I believe he never would have written a single word. His writings have been misinterpreted and twisted by churchmen almost since the time they were penned, so much so that now they are being used as proof texts to say something diametrically opposed to what their intent originally was. Anyone who thinks that Sha'ul taught people not to live according to the *Torah* only does so because that's what they want to think, not because it is what he said. Even on his ministry trips he was instructing the Gentiles to pattern their lives after the instructions of God. Consider these two examples, one from Acts and the other from Galatians:

When Sha'ul and Silas were in Philippi, they were dragged before the magistrates and the accusation raised against them was

> *"These men, being Jews, exceedingly trouble our city; and* ***they teach customs which are not lawful for us, being Romans, to observe.***¹⁵ *"* (emphasis mine)

It is obvious that Sha'ul and Silas were teaching more than just a change of *life* to the Philippians; they were teaching a change of *lifestyle*. The Greek word translated as 'customs' is also used in Acts 6:14 where Stephen is being accused by the Jewish crowd of changing *"the customs which Moses delivered to us."*

In Galatians 2:11-14 we have the infamous confrontation between Sha'ul and Peter (*Kefa* is his Hebrew name). In the heat of the encounter, Sha'ul says to him,

> *"If you being a Jew, live in the manner of the Gentiles and not as the Jews, why do you compel the Gentiles to live as Jews?"*

Good question, right? However this is a very biased selection for the wording of his rebuke. Even in the notes in the margin of my Bible it says that the most respected manuscripts do not say *"**Why do you** compel the Gentiles to live as Jews?"* Instead,

---

¹⁵ Acts 16:20-21

Sha'ul's challenge to Kefa was, *"How can you compel the Gentiles to live as Jews?"* This puts a whole new light on the reason for the confrontation. Sha'ul is not rebuking Kefa for teaching the Gentiles to follow the lifestyle of the Jews; he is rebuking him because Kefa is not living the lifestyle he should be living. Sha'ul is saying, in essence, "How are they ever going to learn to live correctly if you, of all people, aren't setting an example? *You* are supposed to be the example for *them*; instead you have started to be influenced by their ways."

Weighing the evidence

The small amount of evidence I have presented in this chapter, when allowed to speak for itself, unmistakably confirms that Yeshua's followers considered the *Torah* to be the central element of their commission. If what we think the New Testament says does not line up with the message of the *Torah*, then we are thinking wrongly. The Bible delivers the same guidelines from beginning to end; it is due to man's unwillingness to accept this truth that believers today are so far adrift from the course.

Conclusion

The teachings and instructions of God—His *Torah*—are the revelation of the will of God to mankind. They are the way of the LORD, the Truth, the path of righteousness; they are the Tree of Life. Yeshua came to pay the price for our disobedience and to show us how to live according to the will of God. He came to fill the *Torah* with meaning. He taught His followers to keep the *Torah*, and then sent them out to train people in all the world to keep it too. Before they were commissioned, Yeshua poured out the Holy Spirit on them to enable them and empower them for that task. That is still the mission of the Holy Spirit today in the life of a believer.

The message of the grace and mercy of our heavenly Father is conveyed to mankind through the words of *Torah*. In those words are life, peace and blessings beyond comprehension. The *Torah* is the foundation for knowing and understanding God; it underlies the faith of all the apostles, prophets and kings who walked in His presence. Most importantly, the *Torah* is the framework within which and upon which the whole of the New Testament is based; all of the writers emphatically held to its guidelines. This vital truth has been kept from believers for centuries, and is vehemently opposed by many in mainline Christianity today. When examined, the influence behind this cover-up is exposed to be a root of anti-Semitism that sprang up early in the post-apostolic era of the Church.

It is my sincere hope and prayer that all who read this book will seriously consider what I have presented and search it out on their own. It is not my intention to offend those of you who hold dearly to your Christian faith; but if your belief system has been shaken, then you cannot ignore my assault on these long-held façades of the Church. You must not let it rest until you have resolved these issues for yourself.

My conclusion is the same as that of Solomon after he had searched the whole world for the meaning and significance of life. He closed the book of Ecclesiastes with these words:

Let us hear the conclusion of the whole matter:
Fear God and keep His commandments,
For this applies to everyone.

Bibliography

Bacchiocchi, Samuelle; *God's Festivals in Scripture and History* Vol. 1 (Berrien Springs, Biblical Perspectives, 1995)

ben Mordechai, Avi; *Messiah, Vol 1: Understanding His life and Teachings in Hebraic Context* (Millennium 7000, 1997)

Bivin, David and Blizzard, Roy Jr.; *The Difficult Words of Jesus* (Shippensburg, Destiny Image, 1994)

Cairns, Earle E.; *Christianity Through the Centuries* (Grand Rapids, Zondervan, 1954)

Eusebius' Ecclesiastical History (Peabody, Hendrickson Publishers, 1998)

Gibbons, Cardinal James; *The Faith of Our Fathers Being a Plain Exposition and Vindication of the Church Founded by Our Lord Jesus Christ* (Baltimore, John Murray, 1905)

Harris, R. Laird (ed.); *Theological Wordbook of the Old Testament* (Chicago, Moody Press, 1980)

Hislop, Alexander; *The Two Babylons* (Neptune, Loizeaux Brothers, 2nd ed., 1959)

Martin, Dr. Walter; *The Kingdom of the Cults* (Minneapolis, Bethany House Publishers, revised and expanded edition, 1985)

Martin, Ernest L.; *Secrets of Golgotha* (Alhambra, ASK Publications, 1988)

Pennock, Michael; *This is Our Faith: Correlated & Referenced to the Catechism of the Catholic Church* (Ave Maria Press, 1998)

Philips, John; *Exploring the World of the Jew* (Chicago, Moody Press, 1927, rev. 1981)

Reves, Richard M.; *Too Long in the Sun* (Charlotte: Partakers Publications, 2001)

Spong, John Shelby; *Liberating the Gospels; Reading the Bible with Jewish Eyes* (New York, Harper Collins, 1996)

Stern, David H.; *Jewish New Testament Commentary* (Clarksville, Jewish New Testament Publications, 1992)

Thayer, Joseph Henry; *Thayer's Greek-English Lexicon of the New Testament* (Grand Rapids, Zondervan, 1975)

Trimm, James S.; *Hebraic-Roots Version "New Testament"* (Hurst Tx., The Society for the Advancement of Nazarene Judaism, 2001)

Vine, W.E; *Vine's Expository Dictionary of New Testament Words* (MᶜLean, MacDonald Publishing Co.)

Wilson, Marvin R.; *Our Father Abraham*; *Jewish Roots of the Christian Faith* (Grand Rapids, William B. Eerdmans Publishing Co., 1989)

A Selected Bibliography of books on the Feasts of the LORD

Bacchiocchi, Samuelle; *God's Festivals in Scripture and History, 2 Vols.* (Berrien Springs, Biblical Perspectives, 1995)

Chumney, Edward; *The Seven Festivals of the Messiah* (Shippensburg, Destiny Image, 1994)

Fuchs, Daniel; *Israel's Holy Days in Type and Prophecy* (Neptune, Loizeaux Brothers, 1985)

Glaser, Mitch and Glaser, Zhava; *The Fall Feasts of Israel* (Chicago, Moody Press 1987)

Hagee, John; *His Glory Revealed* (Nashville, Thomas Nelson Puiblishing, 1999)

Howard, Kevin and Rosenthal, Martin; *The Feasts of the LORD* (Nashville, Thomas Nelson Publishing, 1997)

Litvin, Danny; *Pentecost is Jewish* (Orange, Promise Publishing Co., 1987)